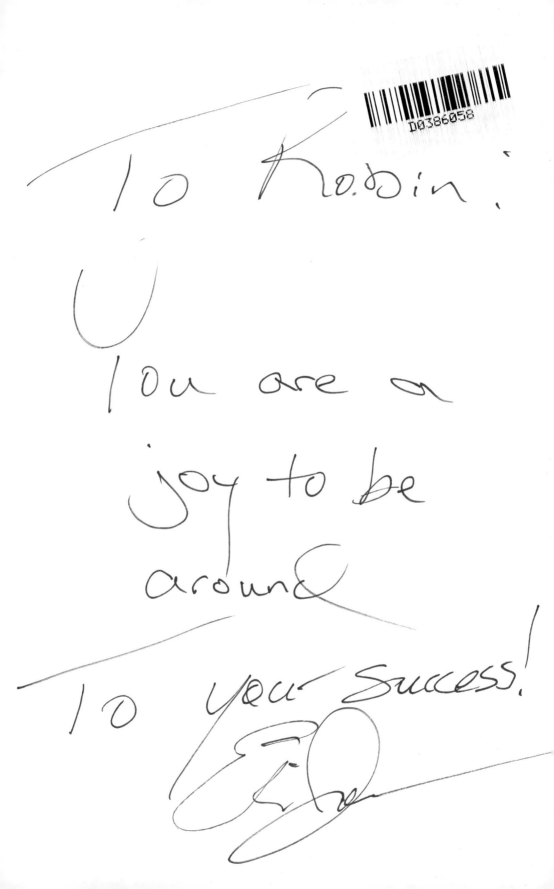

To Robin:

You are a
joy to be
around

To your success!

"One thing is certain in the world of selling—change. *Selling ASAP* is a dynamic book that not only gives you the essential keys to being successful over a long sales career, but also the specific components of mastering sales success in a rapidly changing sales environment. When you devour this book, get out your highlighter and pay special attention to the section on Agility. If you do this, and apply what you learn, your bank account will thank you! Sales managers, if your team is stuck and struggling, understanding Agility can be the difference maker in your performance this year. Read it now!"

   —Tom Ziglar, CEO of Zig Ziglar

"This book belongs in the briefcase of every sales professional, manager, and parent who wants to harness the powers of persuasion and do so in an ethical manner."

   —Robert L. Jolles, author of *Customer Centered Selling* and *Mental Agility: The Path to Persuasion*

"We at Insperity have adopted the philosophy and truths that are found in *Selling ASAP*. We have learned from our clients that a 'trusted advisor' sounds more permanent to them than a sales rep or consultant. Dr. Jones presents a clear road map for serious professionals to become a 'trusted advisor,' helping customers attain even greater success because of their involvement in their business. It is what the 'best' customers now expect."

   —Jay E. Mincks, executive vice president of sales and marketing at Insperity

"I am excited to recommend *Selling ASAP: Art, Science, Agility, Performance*. This book is unique in that it covers the best practices and is backed by solid research. I am certain it will positively impact the skills of professional salespeople who want to reach the next level of sales productivity."

   —Bryan Flanagan, founder of Flanagan Training Group

"If the debate about whether selling is an art or science hasn't been settled, Eli Jones has taken care of that with his important new work, *Selling ASAP: Art, Science, Agility, Performance*. We're not in Kansas anymore, Toto; it's the second decade of the twenty-first century and the urgency of this marketplace is unforgiving of the unprepared. The proven techniques you will acquire in this book will prepare you for twenty-first-century sales success. The question is, are you prepared to risk what you know for what you might learn?"

—Jim Blasingame, host of *The Small Business Advocate Show*

"Dr. Jones and his colleagues do a masterful job of outlining the technical aspects of selling, the 'Science,' but equally as impressive they clearly articulate the value and importance of the 'Art,' noting the importance of 'creativity and spontaneity.' In today's fast-paced world, buyers and prospects are constantly bombarded with people who suggest that they have breakthrough solutions but who often fall short. *Selling ASAP* prescribes the 'secret sauce,' empathy and service, which are critical components for a successful career in sales. This book is a must-read for any serious sales person."

—Dennis R. Maple, president of ARAMARK Education

"I travel the world stressing the need to invest in creating a culture of preparedness. *Selling ASAP* likewise emphasizes preparation as the key to success in sales. The techniques in this book will better prepare you for building solid business relationships that will improve your chances of becoming a trusted advisor. This is a must-read!"

—Lieutenant General Russel Honoré, U.S. Army (Retired)

Selling ASAP

Selling *ASAP*

Art, Science, Agility, Performance

Professional Edition

ELI JONES

LARRY CHONKO

FERN JONES

CARL STEVENS

Louisiana State University Press

Baton Rouge

Published by Louisiana State University Press
Copyright © 2012 by Louisiana State University Press
All rights reserved
Manufactured in the United States of America
First printing

Designer: Laura Roubique Gleason
Typeface: Minion Pro
Printer: McNaughton & Gunn, Inc.
Binder: Acme Bookbinding

Library of Congress Cataloging-in-Publication Data

Selling ASAP : art, science, agility, performance / Eli Jones . . . [et al.]. — Professional ed.
    p.   cm.
  Prev. ed. entered under Jones, Eli.
  Includes bibliographical references and index.
  ISBN 978-0-8071-4427-5 (cloth : alk. paper) — ISBN 978-0-8071-4428-2 (pdf) —
ISBN 978-0-8071-4429-9 (epub) —ISBN 978-0-8071-4430-5 (mobi)
  1. Selling. 2. Sales management. I. Jones, Eli. II. Jones, Eli. Selling ASAP.
  HF5438.25.J658 2012
  658.85—dc23
                              2011037854

Thanks to the Lord for unfailing love and faithfulness, and for blessing us with our most cherished relationships.

To Elvira and Eli Jones, Jr., and Albertine and Bernard Walker. We are inspired by the way you shaped our world.

And to our legacy, our children and grandchildren. We are rewarded by the way you are shaping the future. It is your love that sustains us.

—Eli and Fern Jones

To my wife, Barbara. I have been blessed by her love, her devotion, and her patience. To my children, to whom I hope I have imparted some of the wisdom taught to me by my parents. May they have the same hope with their children. And to my parents, who continue to love me and my family, and who teach me much to this day.

—Larry Chonko

To the best sale I ever made, my childhood and lifetime sweetheart, Miss Jean. You are my inspiration eternally.

—Carl Stevens

Contents

Foreword

Selling ASAP: Art, Science, Agility, Performance is a recipe book for how to achieve your sales objectives by better anticipating prospects' and clients' wants and needs, and by prescribing solutions that build value over time. Personal selling is experiencing a dramatic shift due to radically changing customer expectations. Customers want trusted advisors and not just product experts. They want value and not just performance. They want solutions and not just products.

In a recent study on experts-for-hire versus trusted advisors, which examined clients who are loyal to a supplier versus clients who treat suppliers as vendors, I found significant differences in what clients are looking for in a relationship with sales executives.

Issue	Clients Who Are Loyalists	Clients Who Are at Risk
My service provider . . .		
Has the best interest of the client in mind	92%	51%
Does everything possible to make us successful	87	42
Makes me look good	85	38
Is a leader in his/her field	82	41
Adapts his/her experience to our circumstances	79	43
Is open to feedback to improve performance	76	38

The results are dramatic. The study suggests that in order to become a trusted advisor, salespeople are required to have the best interest of the client in mind; do everything possible to make the client successful; be thought of as a leader in the field; and be adaptable and open to feedback. *Selling ASAP* builds on these ideas, providing step-by-step instructions on how to build a loyal client base and become a trusted advisor in the sales profession. This can be done by using the art and science of selling, being agile and adaptable, and focusing on performance metrics that put the prospect/customer/client front and center of the salesperson's activities.

In *Selling ASAP,* the authors bridge sound academic research and solid business practices to create a unique book on how to build a successful business in sales. Set a goal to become a trusted advisor for your clients, who will then become repeat customers and produce referrals. Trusted advisors search out the primary motivations behind customers' buying practices, provide sound solutions to their clients' business problems, and give consistent, quality customer service after the sale.

I am pleased to recommend *Selling ASAP.* It explains the art and science of professional selling in a fresh, innovative way.

Jagdish N. Sheth, Ph.D.
Charles H. Kellstadt Professor of Marketing
Emory University
Author of *Clients for Life* (Simon & Schuster)

Selling ASAP

1 *Selling ASAP*

If people like you they'll listen to you, but if they trust you they'll do
business with you.
　　　—Zig Ziglar

Research in client perceptions of the best salespeople—those who
have earned the all-important *trusted advisor* status—concludes
the following. The best salespeople have a good understanding of
their clients' industries, ask great questions, are great listeners and "honest
brokers," and continually offer insights and solutions to their customers'
business problems. Do your customers ask you for advice and respect your
judgment about issues that extend beyond your professional expertise? If
someone were to ask a group of your customers who they truly trust to provide ongoing solutions to their business problems, would you be on their
list? Would you be in their inner circle?

With so many sales jobs available, why do so few salespeople succeed
and so many others fail? What are the best practices in selling today? How
can one obtain trusted advisor status in the eyes of the customer? These are
a few of the questions that we attempt to answer as we provide a set of sure-
fire recipes for sales success. This book is designed for people interested in
joining the sales profession and for those who have had moderate success
in sales but want to do better.

What Is Selling ASAP?

The title of this book is *Selling ASAP: Art, Science, Agility, Performance*.
Some say that selling is the art of persuasion, but selling is both a creative
and an analytical process. Creativity and spontaneity are keys to helping
customers find better solutions to their problems. Deduction, observation,

and analytical skills are very important in professional sales, as they are in any science. The marketplace, business in general, and the sales profession are constantly changing, and creativity, critical thinking, and agility are needed to adapt to these changes. When selling is done ethically and sincerely, the salesperson becomes a trusted advisor to a client—a salesperson who listens, can be trusted, is objective, and can offer useful advice. *Selling ASAP* is a reflection of how selling is viewed today as both an art and a science, with an emphasis on practicing agility to enhance performance.

ASAP: Art

The first *A* in *ASAP* stands for *art*. Selling involves your unique style (art) of applying a systematic process (science) to understanding customers' needs and wants and matching the benefits of your product or service to their explicit and sometimes hidden (latent) desires.

Understanding How Buyers Buy

Understanding the uniqueness of each prospect/customer and how to adapt your communication and behavior to that prospect's preferences is the subject of Chapter 2. It lays the foundation for the rest of the chapters.

In order to motivate a customer to buy a product or service, you must empathize with the customer and understand how your customer's mind works. Take a moment to think about the reasons why *you* buy products and services. Are you always rational about your purchase decisions? Do you sometimes buy impulsively, based on emotion? Now think about the purchasing process as a salesperson. How do you appeal to your customers' sometimes rational and sometimes irrational desires to buy?

The focus of this book is on business-to-business selling—in other words, selling to not-for-profit and for-profit organizations. People who buy for organizations are often thought to be rational about what they buy, but they are people with emotions and impulses, just like everyone else. Skillful salespeople understand that in order to influence someone, they must be able to uncover the prospect's latent needs or wants and motivate the prospect to want to fulfill those needs or wants with the salesperson's product, service, and/or ideas. Skillful salespeople also recognize that the power of influence rests in the salesperson's ability to provide continuous value to customers, engage in long-term relationships with them, and adapt to their changing needs and preferences.

The following chapter discusses the importance of knowing customers—from who they are to how they buy—as well as the psychology of human behavior as it relates to buying. We provide specific methods to help you understand the thought processes of your prospects and discern their buying preferences—things that are necessary for salespeople today if they are to succeed in sales.

ASAP: Science

The *S* in *ASAP* stands for *science*. Selling is a science because there are proven systematic methods that work. Selling revolves around the marketing concepts of segmenting and targeting potential customers, and then presenting your products or service to the right prospects at the right time. Chapters 3–8 uncover the science of selling. Each chapter builds on the previous one to delineate a scientific process that, when done correctly, will raise your probability of success in completing a business transaction and beginning the journey to a long-term, mutually beneficial business relationship with your new customer.

What Is Professional Selling?

Some people think of salespeople as being pushy and manipulative. To them, the word *selling* has negative connotations. It implies that someone (a salesperson) forces someone else (a prospect) to do something against that person's will. Some people believe that salespeople are fast-talkers with only one goal in mind: to take their prospect's money. People often say they feel pressured by salespeople, but think about that for a moment. When you last bought something from a salesperson, did that salesperson force you to buy it, or did you have an underlying need or want even before you interacted with the salesperson? Salespeople cannot force a prospect or customer to do anything; the prospect or customer must have some desire.

This book will demonstrate that salespeople who strive to build long-term relationships with customers cannot afford to be pushy, fast-talking, or manipulative. A focus on long-term customer relationships requires salespeople to adopt a lifetime view of their customers.

Taking a Lifetime View of Customers

Professional selling today requires taking a long-term view of customer relationships. The four facets of lifetime customer relationships are:

1. *Product holdings.* The products a customer has purchased and the products the customer currently has on hand.
2. *Product use.* How the customer uses the product and what value the customer derives from using it.
3. *Contacts.* The nature of the sales organization and the salesperson's contacts with the decision-making unit of a client-company over time.
4. *Events.* Occurrences in the life of the customer (e.g., birth of a child, new business opportunities, a change in competitive activity, etc.).

When salespeople collect and use information about these four facets of customer lifetime relationships, they are able to answer questions such as: How many customers have purchased product A? How many customers have purchased it more than once? What is the frequency of contact with customers? Which customers are most profitable? What events occurred prior to losing a customer? What customers purchase which products? What events typically precede purchases?

THOUGHTWARE

When salespeople can answer questions such as these, they put themselves in a better position to create, maintain, and grow lifetime relationships with customers. A key part of building customer relationships is, simply stated, truly knowing your customers. You must think of customers as partners in collaborative relationships designed for maximizing value to both the customer and you and your organization over the long term. Thus, you must develop *thoughtware* about your customers. Thoughtware represents the thinking process salespeople use as they continuously learn about their customers. For example, customers are often grouped by types of relationships, which provides the following advantages:

- Identification of significant events in the life of the customer.
- Avoidance of unneeded duplication of effort.

- Knowledge of loyalty patterns based on the type of relationship established with individual customers.
- Identification of cross-sell opportunities (i.e., finding additional products or services that can provide added value to current customers).
- Identification of up-sell opportunities (working with customers to upgrade existing products or services for the purpose of providing added customer value and solidifying relationships).

Customer lifetime value is not just a forecasting technique or a software package, but a way of thinking about and doing business with customers that emphasizes up-front preparation and profitable long-term relationships. Such long-term relationships are less costly than those formed under the traditional model, which emphasizes single transactions with customers and closing sales.

A Customer-Focused Selling Framework

Figure 1.1 demonstrates how salespeople interact both with customers and people within their selling organizations. The middle row represents the sales process. Briefly, the steps of the sales process are as follows:

- *Preparation.* How to identify prospects with a high probability of buying what you are selling, determine what they need and want, and why they need and want it.
- *Attention.* How to gain initial interest by making a positive first impression and getting the prospect to focus on your business proposition.
- *Examination.* How to ask the right questions in a powerful sequence to determine a specific customer's primary concerns (what the customer wants) and the customer's dominant buying urge (why the customer wants it).
- *Prescription.* How to present a solution that demonstrates your understanding of the customer's situation, problems, needs, and wants, which can either forge a new business relationship or strengthen an existing one.
- *Conviction and Motivation.* How to handle objections by effectively answering prospects' concerns and encouraging customers to purchase through the presentation of value.

- *Completion and Partnering.* How to finalize the arrangements for the sale of a product or service that possesses competitive value in a manner that will delight the customer and lead to a long-term business relationship.

FIGURE 1.1 A Customer-Focused Sales Framework

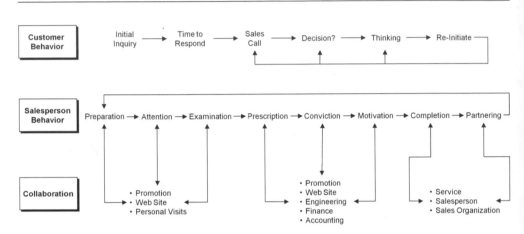

Here is an example of the sales process in action. A customer may tender an inquiry to the sales organization (e.g., a request for proposal, or RFP), or the selling organization may be proactive by engaging in marketing efforts targeted to certain prospects. An inquiry by the prospect may be answered by the salesperson, who initiates *preparation* activity, or by the promotion department, which sends materials via the Internet or invites the customer to peruse the sales organization's website. Whatever the method of contact, the data obtained about the customer should be stored in the sales organization's customer relationship management (CRM) system.

The sales organization can maintain communications with customers through face-to-face meetings, email, websites, social media, telephone calls, or regular mail. One goal of getting the customer's *attention* is to learn more about their unique situation. The salesperson initiates an appointment with the prospect to undertake an *examination* of the prospect's situation and to customize a solution that delivers value. Meanwhile, the prospect may be seeking more information from the sales organization's website or from other vendors. The salesperson does more homework to develop a *prescription* for the prospect's particular situation and makes a sales presentation to show the prospect how the sales organization can satisfy the prospect's short- and long-term needs. During the presentation, the salesperson builds buyer *conviction* about the value of the product or service and *motivates* the prospect to begin a relationship with the sales organization (the step referred to in this book as *conviction and motivation*). Ultimately, the salesperson's goal is to *complete* a transaction and begin a long-term relationship with the prospect as a *partner* (the *completion and partnering* stage).

Sales organizations should utilize a Sales Force Automation (SFA) or Customer Relationship Management (CRM) system to record all customer contacts so that various members of the sales organization (e.g., sales support) will have access to the information. Even when a prospect does not purchase initially, the sales organization should record all relevant information (name, method of contact, reasons for not buying, etc.) so that the organization's salespeople can use this valuable information in their attempts to create long-term relationships with other customers as well as with this one. Such business functions have been the hallmark of many marketing activities for decades. What is new is *how* salespeople are collaborating with each other, their customers, and other sales organization members to accomplish these marketing functions.

ASAP: Agility

The second *A* in *ASAP* stands for *agility,* a key component in selling today. Agility is dynamic, context-specific, change-embracing, and growth-oriented. Agility requires salespeople to be in continuous readiness for change.[1] In today's rapidly shifting business and customer environment, being agile is important.

The definition of agile is nimble, light and quick in motion, active and swift. *Agility* is defined as the ability to thrive in an environment of continuous change. An agile sales force is one that is quick to see opportunities, shrewd in developing short sales-cycle strategies, able to meet customers' individual needs, and capable, flexible, and fast at learning and unlearning. To become agile, you should strive to become as innovative as possible. One measure of agility is your ability to customize your product/service offerings to customers' individual needs, both in the first transaction and throughout the business relationship. Agile salespeople can differentiate themselves to customers by integrating information from the sales organization and the business environment and garnering support from those in the sales organization.

The underlying theme of agility selling is the need to change and learn in order to stay up-to-date with changing market conditions. Salespeople must change what they do if they are to keep up with customers' needs and wants. Traditionally, salespeople have been responsible for activities revolving around the selling of products and services to customers. Today, however, the role of the salesperson is becoming much more broad as salespeople endeavor to incorporate a CRM focus.

Salespeople should not limit their thinking or their sales approaches. Agile salespeople continually analyze how things can be done better. A major challenge for salespeople is coping with information and making decisions in such a dynamic environment. How quickly can you adapt to a changing environment? Research shows that being "street smart" can facilitate selling in today's business environment.

Street Smarts

Salespeople who are street smart achieve a good fit between themselves and their environment.[2] Street smarts, also known as contextual intelligence, consists of the following skills:

1. *Adaptation.* Achieving of a good fit between oneself and one's environment. Adaptive salespeople are adept at reading prospects' underlying motives and goals, nonverbal cues, and emotions, and they are able to respond appropriately.
2. *Environment selection.* Choosing an environment that makes the most of one's talents and abilities. Salespeople have considerably greater control over their job environment than they might think. Choice of employer is one avenue of control. Choice of sales territory assignment can be another. Within a sales territory, salespeople can choose the customers on whom they want to focus.
3. *Environmental shaping.* Altering aspects of one's environment to bring them more in line with one's talents and abilities. Salespeople who can shape the values and priorities of their immediate supervisor, support staff, and upper management are in a position to be more successful than those who cannot.

Salespeople are boundary-spanners. You interact with people outside your company (e.g., customers and competitors) as well as with other employees inside it. As such, you are in position to gather information that can help your sales organization considerably in making managerial decisions. Through a prudent use of this informational power, you can impress management and significantly alter management's values and priorities. Also, because you interact with many customers, you are in a position to shape your customers' values and priorities. Two means for affecting customers' preferences are being prudent about what to say to customers and when to say it, and offering creative suggestions for how customers can solve their business problems.

Street smarts combined with agility selling can lead to improvements in sales performance.

The Four O's of Agility Selling

Today, more than ever, sales companies and individual salespeople need to be agile at both the personal and organizational levels in order to thrive in a world of continuous change. In his book *Business Blindspots,* Benjamin Gilad says:

> Competitiveness is based on learning, which is based on the ability to listen: to customers, to consumers, to partners such as suppliers, or to competitors, to industry experts, and, most important, to one's own employees. The essence of this philosophy is so simple it is embarrassing. The competitive environment sends messages all the time: signals about change, trends, prospects, threats, and weaknesses. Early on, these signals are weak, ambiguous, and hidden. Tapping them and then learning from them is an art that requires open eyes, ears, and minds.[3]

One characteristic of agile salespeople is their ability to successfully disrupt the status quo—not necessarily causing chaos, but getting those around them to think outside the proverbial box. Agile salespeople must be skillful at implementing the following four Os:[4]

- *Observe.* Pay close attention to customers and competitors, and continually look for ways to improve individual and company performance.

- *Orient.* Think about how your observations will affect current and future business.
- *Opt.* Decide which issues to pursue, based on your observations, and how to pursue them with the appropriate support people in the sales organization.
- *Orchestrate.* Act! Don't procrastinate. Time is of the essence in agility selling. Often, major account salespeople are looked upon to orchestrate and lead the sales and support activities of the selling organization to anticipate and meet key accounts' needs.

In a business context, salespeople who can perform this sequence faster than their competitors become more attractive to customers and can achieve a competitive advantage. Too often, salespeople base their decisions on a limited, out-of-date knowledge base built on previous experience. In a fast-moving business landscape, this is a dangerous practice; what worked well last year may no longer be applicable today. You need to have up-to-date intelligence—that is, knowledge and experience—to use as the basis for your decisions.

The Need for Speed [5]

Speed in decision-making is becoming vitally important. Response time is critical to customers and directly reflects how customers perceive an organization's customer service. Salespeople should aim at making their products/services more attractive to the ultimate judges—current customers and potential new customers. Every time a customer decides to buy something, a competitive assessment takes place. Customers do not necessarily take the lowest-priced product or service; rather, they look for what they *perceive* will give them the best value and/or best meet their short- and long-term needs. Every sale, therefore, is made against some competitive force. Just as profit can be a byproduct of success, rather than an end in itself, a salesperson's agility can have an impact on competitors, even when that is not the primary goal.

Agility is a concept useful to all salespeople. To be agile, you must be adept at identifying the different levels of change that will confront you. When facing change, be adaptable in such a way as to employ organizational resources to offer workable solutions to customers' business problems. However, you must also be agile in the sense that you are creative in applying organizational resources, with speed, to customize solutions that solve short-term problems while simultaneously thinking of the longer term.

Customer Expectations

These days, customer expectations and preferences are ever-changing and ever-increasing. In particular, customer expectations are increasing in relation to salesperson knowledge, speed of response, breadth and depth of communication, and customization of information, products, and services. As customers expect more, successful salespeople are no longer able to use the first sales call to gather information that can be obtained using other readily available sources, such as what is in the public domain online. Technological advances have increased the expectations of customers regarding how—and how quickly—salespeople respond. Customers expect customized solutions and, indeed, co-created solutions that best meet their needs. These rising expectations are a part of increased market turbulence. Market turbulence is the rate of change in the composition of customers and their preferences. Sales organizations operating in turbulent markets are likely to have to modify their products and services continually in order for salespeople to adapt satisfactorily to customers' changing preferences. With rapid market change, salespeople face a constant challenge to learn new products, new sales techniques, and new sales strategies, and they may have to unlearn old sales strategies that are no longer viable.

In these changing times, you must ask yourself the following questions: Am I becoming obsolete in any way? Or could this be the time in my career when I am ready to embrace change and perform at a higher level?

Competitive Advantage

Agility is a way of competing. For firms to be agile, their workforces must be agile. For the agile salesperson, agility is not something that just happens. It is *made* to happen. Agile salespeople learn when they take time to examine how things are done, and they do not wait for problems to emerge or for customers to indicate they have changed their needs or preferences. Agile salespeople continuously reflect on what they do, how they do it, and why they do it. Such reflection becomes a behavioral norm that enables agile salespeople to question assumptions and seek out solutions to problems. Agile salespeople also recognize that agility is not the culmination of a process. Rather, it is a process. Agility will always change because marketplace changes are always occurring.

Agility is a trainable skill. Salespeople can learn the types of change and how to respond proficiently. They can learn to offer, quickly, solutions to unanticipated change. Agility is based on knowledge levels, on a willingness to learn, and on various organizational support activities that should be forthcoming if the organization aspires to be agile. A fascinating aspect of agility is that its meaning is ever-changing. Agility is about responding to the unexpected with speed. Responding to the unanticipated requires unplanned responses that might extend the frontiers of sales practice.

Access to knowledge about customers and the business environment is a critical factor in developing agility. The knowledge stored in a sales organization's databases and in a salesperson's memory is the lifeblood of agility. A salesperson's ability to manage, analyze, and communicate information to customers is a base requirement for survival. But it is also a source of competitive advantage, especially if it allows salespeople to reduce the time needed to proceed from observation of problem situations to orchestration of customer-focused solutions.

ASAP: Performance

The *P* in *ASAP* stands for *performance*. You must consistently perform at a high level over a long period of time. Sales performance has been a requirement of the profession from the very beginning. What is different now is the multitude of ways in which sales performance is measured. Selling is not just about making sales or achieving a quota; it is also about an emphasis on continuous learning and on maintaining long-term customer satisfaction and customer loyalty. It is about becoming the customer's trusted advisor.

Measuring Sales Performance

Given the rapidity of change, the increased need for learning, and the need for building long-term relationships with customers, selling, in a sense, has changed. As sales organizations emphasize customer relationships, many aspects of the sales job—including customer satisfaction, sales growth, new product success, and profitability—are taking on more importance as salesperson performance measures. Table 1.1 lists some performance measures being used today by sales organizations. For sales companies that are learning-oriented, traditional outcome-based measures of performance, shown on the right side of Table 1.1, are inadequate.

Sales companies that measure results by employing only outcome-based measurements, such as sales volume, require very little monitoring of salespeople. Little managerial direction is needed, and the measures of results are straightforward. Such companies focus on the results of effort and wait for those results to send signals to salespeople about how they are performing. If the results are inadequate, changes are made. But these outcome-based measures are retrospective, providing little insight into what the salespeople can do *during* the sales cycle to advance the sale and build the business relationship. Thus, little learning occurs. For example, if a salesperson's revenue declines by 10 percent, what corrective action is suggested by the revenue decline? With outcome-based measures, the knowledge that sales are down is restricted to results; these measures reveal nothing about *why* sales are down. Alternatively, behavior-based measures (shown in the left column in Table 1.1)—such as depth and breadth of customer knowledge, new account generation activities, planning, decision-making, and new sales strategies—lead to improved results.

Ethical Codes and Performance

Surprisingly, selling *ethically* is a behavior that has received little attention from those who measure performance. Yet it is a critically important behavior that produces results over a long period of time. Integrity should be your hallmark. Regardless of the excuses salespeople may use to try to explain unethical behavior, there is no substitute for integrity. Developers of ethical codes should consider the performance dimensions for which salespeople are responsible. Standards of behavior concerning performance can be captured in the following three questions:

1. Does the behavior or result achieved comply with organizational standards of behavior as specified in the code of ethics?
2. Does the behavior or result achieved comply with professional standards of behavior as specified in an industry code?
3. Does the behavior or result achieved comply with all applicable laws, regulations, and government codes?

TABLE 1.1 Behavior-Based and Outcome-Based Sales Performance Measures

Behavior-Based Measures	Outcome-Based Measures
• Product knowledge	• Sales volume dollars
• Company knowledge	• Sales volume units
• Organizational commitment	• Gross margin
• Job satisfaction	• Profitability
• Acceptance of authority	• Sales expenses
• Acceptance of performance reviews	• Percent to quota
• Risk-seeking preferences	• Call frequency
• Motivation	
• Planning	
• Sales call activity	
• Selling versus non-selling time	
• Selling harder	
• Selling smarter	
• Information gathering	
• Sales presentation planning	
• Participation in decision-making	

Source: Adapted from Richard L. Oliver and Erin Anderson, "Behavior-Based and Outcome-Based Sales Control Systems: Evidence and Consequences of Pure-Form and Hybrid Governance," *Journal of Personal Selling and Sales Management* 15 (Fall 1995): 1–16.

The Customer-Focused Salesperson

Salespeople who have a customer focus are willing to learn, manage what they learn well, and realize improved results, achieving customer loyalty. The core values of customer focus and knowledge management allow salespeople to provide better customer service, which results in greater customer loyalty, which results in improved dialogue, which results in even better customer service, which results in improved customer loyalty, and so on.

Customer loyalty provides tremendous benefits. One benefit is fewer customer defections, which means fewer lost customers. This also translates into your having more long-term relationships with customers. Both of these things help avoid some of the high costs of finding new customers. Another benefit of customer loyalty is the dialogue that opens between you and your customers. Improved dialogue enables honest discussion and objective feedback from customers, which can help you improve professionally.

What Do You Need to Succeed in Sales?

Successful salespeople possess the following five traits: motivation to succeed, empathy, service motivation, conscientiousness, and ego strength.[6] Each trait is briefly discussed below.

1. *Motivation to succeed (ego-drive)* is the first necessary trait for effective selling. Sales managers often rely too much on external motivation, for example by providing monetary incentives to salespeople. These are usually effective in the short term, but true motivation that causes individuals to excel comes from within. In the long term, what truly makes the difference is internal/intrinsic motivation. There must be an inner drive to be successful.

2. *Empathy* is the second element essential to sales success. Empathy is the ability to sense the reactions of other people and pick up the subtle clues provided by others in order to accurately assess what they are thinking and feeling. Selling, by definition, is an interpersonal interaction. The purpose of this interaction is persuasive communication. Consequently, you must be able to understand buyers—to feel what they feel, to think as they think—in order to sell well.

3. *Service motivation* is described as a motivational force that parallels ego drive. A service-motivated salesperson derives satisfaction from serving and receiving appreciation from others.

4. *Conscientiousness* combines a high level of self-drive with a high degree of responsibility. Conscientious salespeople are driven to accomplish goals and complete tasks as an expression of themselves. They are purposeful, strong-willed, and determined individuals. They practice self-control that results in actively planning, organizing, and carrying out tasks.

5. *Ego strength,* or resilience, is the degree to which an individual likes himself or herself. Successful salespeople have a high degree of ego strength. Failure does not destroy their positive view of themselves. A high degree of ego strength helps a salesperson endure rejection, and selling is replete with rejection. People who are attempting to

persuade other people are more likely to have their ideas rejected than accepted. That is why you must have ego strength. Understand that it is the idea that may be rejected, not you the person.

To truly succeed in a sales profession, you must evolve from being solely a person who possesses the key traits and has selling skills to becoming a trusted business advisor who knows how to sell. Today's sales professionals must have real business acumen. Not only must you know how to read a company's annual report, understand cash flow, and interpret acronyms, but you also must be able to translate this knowledge into an understanding of the business drivers needed to produce a significant return on investment (ROI) for your prospective client, while adding value to your prospect's business proposition.

If you're looking to position yourself above your toughest competition, read this book in its entirety as you continue your journey to true success in *selling . . . ASAP!*

2 *Understanding How Buyers Buy*

> To find out what the customer needs you have to understand what the customer is doing as well as he understands it. Then you build what he needs and you educate him to the fact that he needs it.
>
> —Edna St. Vincent Millay

Uncovering Needs and Wants

In order to make a compelling argument for buying, you need to know how to uncover your prospects' implied and expressed feelings and thoughts about the solution (the product or service) being offered. The information in this chapter builds on the principles of selling ASAP—the art, science, agility, and performance necessary to be successful in sales—by focusing on the psychological aspects of buying and selling. The goal is to enhance your understanding of what your prospects, customers, and clients could be thinking as you present a business solution. With this understanding, you will be able to adapt your communication to suit your customers' preferences and thus better utilize the art of selling.

The Greek philosopher Aristotle said, "All men seek a goal—success or happiness. The only way to achieve true success is to express yourself completely in service to society. First, have a definite, clear, practical idea—a goal, an objective. Second, seek the necessary means to achieve your ends—wisdom, money, materials, and methods. Third, adjust all your means to that end."

The above quote emphasizes that goal setting and goal achieving are aspects of human motivation. You must understand that goals, or personal strivings, are at the heart of buying. Goals determine customers' psychological wants and needs—those inner urges or drives that will motivate customers to action. Part of the selling process is assessing and adapting to the style of the prospect. To motivate a prospect to action, you must understand the goal orientation of that person. The starting point here is motivation, the driving force for all human behavior.

Motivation

Motivation is what moves people into action. More formally, motivation is defined as the state of drive or arousal that impels behavior toward a goal-object. Thus, motivation has two components: (1) drive or arousal, and (2) goal-object. Drive is an internal state of tension that produces actions to reduce that tension. A goal-object is something in the external world whose acquisition will reduce the tension. Arousal or drive provides the energy to act; the goal-object provides the direction for channeling that energy. When energy is expended to attain some goal-object, that use of energy is called purposive behavior.

The Process of Motivation

The motivational process, shown in Figure 2.1, begins when a stimulus engenders arousal or drive. The arousal can be autonomic (felt physiologically), such as when a prospect first realizes an urgent need to cut operating costs and shows signs of stress. It also can be emotive, for example, when a client first learns that she is being promoted on the job and becomes joyful. Or it can be cognitive, such as when a prospect is struggling to find a way out of a deal that she no longer finds attractive and is in thinking mode.[1]

The arousal leads a person to act. Autonomic (physiological) or emotive arousal can elicit the relevant behavior directly. In a business context, when a prospect sees an express mail envelope in the mail, his automatic response is usually to open that envelope first; this is an example of autonomic arousal. An example of emotive arousal is when, because of trust issues, the prospect buys products only from salespeople she knows well. Cognitive arousal also elicits behavior, but generally only after further cognitive activity to figure out possible goal-directed behaviors. For example, a person seeking a way out of a commitment will identify and deliberate on all available options. In business, a new project causes cognitive arousal when a response to a request for proposal must be reviewed and deliberated upon by members of the decision-making unit, often a buying committee.

Following the automatic or selected behavior, the prospect experiences a new state, bringing with it a possible sense of satisfaction. This outcome, if positive, calms the prospect's drive. If the new state is not satisfactory, feedback recycles the process and the prospect keeps searching for an ideal solution.

Persuasion as Motivation

Persuasion is often a necessary motivator in selling. Persuasion means influencing opinions or affecting attitudes by means of communication—not only by informing, but also by educating and motivating. It involves affecting the hearts as well as the minds of people.

To persuade a person, the message has to reach the prospect's emotions, not merely the person's sense of logic. Choices are made emotionally much more frequently than rationally. Buyers make decisions in the marketplace, sometimes consciously but frequently unconsciously, and generally are not aware of what motivates them to buy because they are not always conscious of their own wants. Sometimes the prospect's underlying feelings manifest themselves in the form of hidden objections, which are discussed later in

FIGURE 2.1 Model of the Motivation Process

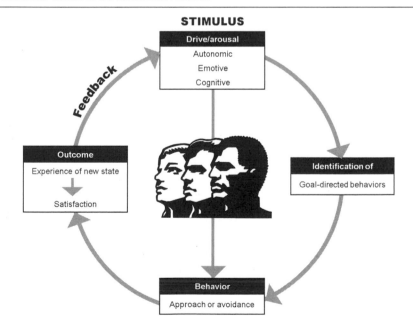

this book. As a trusted advisor, you should seek a complete understanding of your prospects' goals in order to help them achieve *their* goals. When you do, your prospects will become satisfied and loyal clients—people who have achieved what they wanted.

Need Arousal

The product benefits that buyers seek and their attitudes toward various product options are referred to as the psychological set, which is dynamic. It changes during decision-making as new information is processed. The benefits customers seek and their attitudes are a function of the following:

1. *Past experiences* with the salesperson's product or a competitive product.
2. *The buyer's personal characteristics,* such as demographics, lifestyle, and personality.
3. *The buyer's motives/drives,* which define the buyer's needs and direct behavior toward fulfilling those needs.
4. *Environmental influences,* such as culture, social class, others in the decision-making unit, or the buying situation.
5. *Past marketing stimuli,* including product, price, and promotion directed to the buyer and his company.

You can influence the buyer's need arousal, and thus influence this process, by understanding the buyer's personality characteristics and business and personal goals, probing to fully uncover needs and wants, and providing new information about products and services, economic conditions, and advertising claims. You can influence information processing by making sure that the information you provide is relevant to the benefits the buyer seeks, and also conforms to the buyer's beliefs and attitudes.

Arousal-Seeking Buying Behavior

One of the human needs that underlies buying experiences is the need for arousal. Humans have an innate need for an optimal level of stimulation, which is the level at which a person feels neither bored nor overwhelmed.

When prospects first encounter a new idea, they become interested, and the idea holds their attention. However, as they continue to be exposed to the idea, they become used to it, or adapt to it. Once they reach their adaptation level of stimulation—that is, the level of stimulation that is perceived as normal or average—they lose interest in the new idea. If your ideas are all within the adaptation level, they will arouse no interest, and the prospect will be starved of stimulation. If, in contrast, prospects become exposed to too many new ideas (e.g., from many different salespeople), they will become overwhelmed and stressed and will either spontaneously act to shut down or else decide to continue with what they are currently doing. Conversely, when the stimulation falls below the optimal level, prospects will feel bored and will seek more stimulating experiences.[2]

You need to approach prospects enthusiastically with new ideas (potential solutions) to address their business problems. You can differentiate yourself from competitors by being sensitive to prospects' optimal level of stimulation. You can do this by paying close attention to when you have a prospect's interest and when you are losing it. Being sensitive to *verbal and nonverbal cues* is one way for you to determine the prospect's level of interest.

The arousal-seeking motive is a person's internal drive to maintain stimulation at an optimal level. Some people are more arousal-seeking and generally more risk-taking than others. Arousal-seeking people tend to adopt new products and switch brands just to try out something new. They also look for more information about products and get bored when exposed to repetitive sales presentations. Among business customers, arousal seekers are likely to be open to alternative suppliers' presentations, be predisposed to attend trade shows and professional conferences, and actively search for better products and services.

If the buyer is arousal seeking, you must stay in constant contact with the buyer and present new solutions, new products, and new services in order to maintain the buyer's interest. You must work hard to learn about what is at the core of buying behavior. Not all business customers are the same; accordingly, you must adapt your communication and behavior to buyers' personalities and preferred styles of doing business. This is called *adaptive selling.*

Adaptive Selling

Each buyer has different styles and interests, and therefore each sales presentation you give should be tailored to accommodate those differences. Focusing on each individual's needs and wants requires an understanding of adaptive selling. The practice of adaptive selling is defined as "the altering of sales behaviors during a customer interaction or across customer interactions based on the perceived information about the nature of the selling situation."[3] Adaptive selling entails gathering information about each customer, observing customers' reactions during the sales call, showing agility by making rapid adjustments, and tailoring sales presentations to each customer's preferences, goals, needs, and wants. You are likely to improve your performance if you engage in customer-oriented selling behaviors and alter your sales presentations according to the selling situation.

To adapt your behavior to customer preferences and the nature of the selling situation, you must have a thorough understanding of customers' thoughts and actions. Over the years, salespeople have wondered why people act like they do. What governs or controls human behavior? Sometimes it seems to be beyond logic. This is because, again, human behavior is controlled by both logic *and* emotions. Our actions may not always be sensible, logical, or "right." Salespeople commonly complain about losing sales to competitors with "inferior" products and not understanding why. Often, the reason is that the competitors did a better job of communicating and appealing to the buyer's personal and professional needs. To help you understand this better, the next section examines social styles.

Social Styles Matrix[4]

Research has indicated that each of us is a blend of four distinct personality, or social, types. In adaptive selling, you must adapt your natural style to be more like the prospect's style. By using different sales presentations for different social styles, and altering sales presentations during sales calls to fit the situation and the prospect's style, you will find it easier to get the prospect's attention and, ultimately, share understanding with the prospect.

Knowledge of the prospect's personal communication/social style is a key ingredient in effectively capturing the prospect's attention. A popular method for helping you adapt your communication styles is the social styles matrix (see Figure 2.2). The matrix reflects the fact that people have certain preferred communication behaviors when interacting with one another. As you recognize and adjust to these behavior patterns, you will develop stronger relationships with customers.

Two dimensions in Figure 2.2 are the key to understanding social styles: responsiveness (the side axis) and assertiveness (the bottom axis). These dimensions are discussed in the following sections.

FIGURE 2.2 Social Styles Matrix

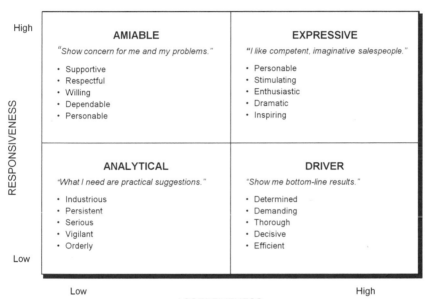

Responsiveness: High / Low (side axis). Assertiveness: Low / High (bottom axis).

AMIABLE
"Show concern for me and my problems."
- Supportive
- Respectful
- Willing
- Dependable
- Personable

EXPRESSIVE
"I like competent, imaginative salespeople."
- Personable
- Stimulating
- Enthusiastic
- Dramatic
- Inspiring

ANALYTICAL
"What I need are practical suggestions."
- Industrious
- Persistent
- Serious
- Vigilant
- Orderly

DRIVER
"Show me bottom-line results."
- Determined
- Demanding
- Thorough
- Decisive
- Efficient

Responsiveness

The first dimension of the social styles matrix is responsiveness, which is the degree to which people show their emotions publicly. Responsive people are more animated and warm, with a tendency to show their emotions more readily than less responsive people. Often they are more people-oriented than task-oriented. Prospects high in responsiveness are quick to show excitement, joy, anger, frustration, and so on during the sales interaction. Less responsive people tend to control their emotions more and may appear to be more serious, cautious, intelligent, and formal. You must adapt quickly to the prospect's emotional demeanor.

Responsive people generally are:

- Friendly
- Talkative
- Approachable
- Less time-sensitive
- Slower decision-makers
- More sensitive to others' feelings

According to Figure 2.2, amiables and expressives tend to be high in responsiveness, while analyticals and drivers tend to be low in responsiveness.

Assertiveness

The second dimension of the matrix is assertiveness, the degree to which people have opinions about issues and make their positions clear to others publicly. Assertive people have a tendency to state their opinions more often than they ask others for their opinions, and they also tend to have a take-charge attitude. In contrast, unassertive people tend to keep their opinions to themselves or share their opinions only with very close friends.

Assertiveness is different from aggressiveness. In sales, assertiveness means responding to customer needs positively with a high degree of self-confidence, while aggressiveness means controlling the sales interaction but ignoring customer needs and concerns. Often, aggressive salespeople fail to ask enough questions to ascertain the prospect's needs, wants, and opinions. You need to be assertive, but not aggressive, in probing for hidden buyer needs while addressing those needs with confidence in the features and benefits of your product or service.

Assertive people generally are:

- Task-oriented
- Competitive
- Rapid movers
- Quick decision-makers
- Initiative takers
- Time-sensitive

Figure 2.2 demonstrates that people who are "expressives" and "drivers" tend to be high in assertiveness, whereas "amiables" and "analyticals" tend to be low in assertiveness. The next section discusses the characteristics of the four social styles in more detail and examines how you can effectively sell to each style.

The Four Social Styles

The lower left quadrant of the matrix in Figure 2.2 describes the social style termed analytical. Analyticals are low in assertiveness *and* responsiveness. They value facts and logic, and they are task-oriented. Analyticals feel they need to make the absolute right decision; therefore, they tend to need more time in the decision cycle. When selling to an analytical, you need to be calm, cool, poised, detailed, and factual. You should not share personal opinions with analyticals but should stick to the facts. You should show analyticals large amounts of evidence from third-party, credible sources (e.g., the *Wall Street Journal, Forbes,* consumer reports, research studies, etc.). If your sales organization has conducted extensive research on its product or service, you should make certain you show analytical prospects the research reports, explaining that your products have been field-tested and found to be in demand. You must be prepared to go into detail with an analytical. If you do not know the answer to an analytical prospect's questions, don't wing it; instead, tell the prospect that you will obtain the information and get back to them within twenty-four hours with the answer.

Found directly above analytical in the matrix is the social style called amiable. Amiables are low in assertiveness and high in responsiveness. They tend to value relationships and cooperation; they are very people-oriented. Amiables operate on mutual respect. Like analyticals, they take more time than some people to make decisions, but this is usually because they strive to build consensus among the people involved in the decision. They dislike conflict and value harmony. When dealing with an amiable, you should demonstrate the impact that the product or service will have on the amiable's people (e.g., job satisfaction, happiness, higher morale, cooperation, etc.) and offer guarantees and testimonials—that is, evidence that other *people* are buying the product or service. Also, you should ask for and use referrals from amiables, emphasizing that long-term relationship selling is part of your goal by assuring the amiable that you will be there for her throughout the decision cycle and after the purchase.

With both analyticals and amiables, you need to slow down and not present to them too quickly. People with these social styles associate fast-talkers with being pushy and manipulative. Because of their tendency to be risk-averse, you will want to involve them in your presentations by focusing your trial close questions on addressing their concerns. For example, you might ask, "Have I properly addressed your concerns about the product's reliability?"

Directly opposite of analyticals, in the upper right quadrant of the matrix in Figure 2.2, is the social style termed expressive. Expressives are high in assertiveness *and* responsiveness. They tend to be approachable and competitive. They value recognition and creativity, and their focus is on the future. Although expressives are task-oriented, they also can be people-oriented. They can be very swift in making decisions. In selling to expressives, you should emphasize how your products or services make them more competitive and keep them on the leading edge. Expressives are more visionary (future-oriented) than the other social styles. With expressives, you need to talk about the future impact that your product or service will have on increasing efficiency and effectiveness. You also need to emphasize the importance of being first in the industry to buy the product or service. Expressives like new and bold ideas. With them, you should find ways to focus on innovation, new products, new services, new styles, and so on. If appropriate, you might give an expressive customer a plaque with his name on it for purchasing your product. If possible, you should write a note to the expressive's boss, thanking the company and the buyer for buying the new and innovative product. Enthusiasm is essential when presenting to an expressive. You must show more excitement for the products or services than you would when presenting to people with the other social styles.

The last social style in the matrix, found in the lower right quadrant, is the driver. Drivers are high in assertiveness and low in responsiveness. They are very task- and bottom-line oriented, and they are efficient decision-makers. With drivers, you must be direct and organized in your presentations and get right to the point. Do not waste a lot of time on chitchat. Drivers value time and efficiency, and they take calculated risks. You need to show them the impact that your product or service will have on profitability, market share, lower costs, and so on; however, merely show them the facts and avoid bogging them down with details. Listen closely to what drivers say. They will make comments like, "So, what's the bottom line?" You might even see some signs of impatience in drivers. For example, if you ramble about something that is not important to a driver, she might rush you to the next point. You must be patient and not take it personally. Directness is part of the driver's personality.

When selling to drivers, you need to be prepared to sell at a fairly quick pace. Involve drivers in your presentations by asking for their opinions about your products or services. You should also ask many trial close questions, such as, "What do you think about the product so far?" Drivers and analyticals respond better to "thinking-type" questions, while expressives and amiables respond better to "feeling-type" questions, such as, "How do you feel about the product so far?"

This social styles classification scheme can help you in adapting your presentations to individual prospects' styles. However, prospects and customers may not fit one style exactly as it is presented here. In general, the business world is fast-paced. A buyer who has an amiable social style off-the-clock may demonstrate driver tendencies at work because he is under deadline pressures. Over time, you really get to know your clients' most prominent social styles through interactions with them, and often you have to revise your first impressions of your clients. The point is for you to use the factors in the classification scheme to adapt to individual buyers.

When selling to a buying committee or decision-making unit, pay attention to the social style that becomes evident during the meeting. Often, the group will succumb to the most dominant person in the room and take on that person's social style. Again, adapt your communication to fit the social style that is most dominant at the time.

Buying-committee member perceptions of different products and companies can be changed, so you must understand why specific perceptions exist and, if they are inaccurate, provide information, testimonials, and other evidence that can change unfavorable perceptions or reinforce favorable ones. You also may be able to adjust the power relationships in the buying committee. For example, in business-to-business sales, it is a best practice for salespeople to leverage an *internal champion,* such as a coach or sponsor—someone who already believes in the merits of the product or service—to do the work of assembling and mobilizing the buying committee within the buying organization.

Perceived Risk

In many sales situations, the most important perception to be dealt with is risk. As you prescribe solutions, you must provide evidence that your solutions will work, reducing perceived risk. Testimonials from satisfied customers are very useful in such circumstances. Furthermore, astute salespeople will leverage relationships with the buying-committee members they know the best and with individuals who can provide support about the integrity of the salesperson and the sales organization.

People with different social styles perceive risks differently, and buyers/prospects face several types of risk in making purchasing decisions:

1. *Financial risk.* This type of risk is a function of the cost of a product relative to available funds. A new company on a very restricted budget will view a nonessential product as very risky compared to a more established company with greater sources of funds.
2. *Social risk.* A purchase may not meet the standards of an important reference group. Customers buy certain products that make favorable impressions on their peer groups. For example, a new technology for the office may appeal to doctors who are making a statement to their peers that they fit in with the group and are successful.
3. *Psychological risk.* A product that is important to the buyer may not conform to the buyer's self-image. Newly promoted purchasing agents, for example, may be very careful in making purchasing decisions in order to show others that they have power and authority.
4. *Performance risk.* The product may not work as anticipated or may fail. This risk is greatest when the product is technically complex or when ego-related needs are involved.
5. *Physical risk.* This is the risk of bodily harm as a result of product performance. For example, salespeople selling new machinery to industrial plants may encounter buyers who are concerned about the extent to which their workers could get hurt while using the equipment.

Selling to Prospects' Needs and Wants

Clearly, the goal in sales is to reach a common understanding between the buyer and the seller. The degree to which someone understands what another person is trying to communicate depends on many factors: how much alike they are; how similar their backgrounds, experiences, language skills, attitudes, and beliefs are; and the assumptions they make about each other based on stereotypes. Remember, your mission is to fully uncover the prospect's wants and needs, and to build creative solutions that fit those wants and needs. Understanding wants is pretty simple. The next section will help you build your knowledge about needs.

Needs

The concept of selling to needs and wants is closely aligned with the concept of motivation. As discussed earlier, a need is a felt deprivation of a desired state. The desired state provides the goal-object, and deprivation of that state provides the drive. Psychologists and consumer researchers have suggested various categories of needs. Among the most relevant to salespeople are Henry Murray's *psychogenic needs* and Abraham Maslow's *needs hierarchy.*

Murray focused on basic needs in personality, which he called psychogenic needs. He believed these needs operate largely at the unconscious level. Table 2.1 is adapted from Murray's list of psychogenic needs.[5]

The social styles discussed earlier can be integrated with Murray's psychogenic needs theory to help you better understand prospects and customers. Analyticals, for example, need autonomy and cognizance (two of Murray's psychogenic needs). They look for solid, tangible, practical evidence to support the validity of their decisions. They also require assurance that their decisions will be valid for the future. Amiables need nurturance and exposition. They place a high priority on friendships, cooperative behavior, and being accepted by others. They frequently stay with the comfortable and known, avoiding risks that could strain their personal relationships. Expressives need autonomy, dominance, exhibition, and exposition. They need creative ideas and recognition. Drivers need autonomy, dominance, and cognizance. They know what they want, where they are going, and are oriented toward getting results. They are fact-oriented and do not need reinforcing feelings or opinions from others.

Maslow's needs hierarchy can also be applied to the concept of selling to needs and wants. In the late 1960s, Maslow developed a hierarchical theory of human needs (see Figure 2.3). Maslow was a humanistic psychologist

TABLE 2.1 Murray's Psychogenic Needs

Need	Definition	Examples
Autonomy	To be independent and free to act according to impulse. To be unattached, irresponsible. To defy convention.	Impulse buying. Wearing unconventional clothing.
Dominance	To direct the behavior of others.	Aggressively demanding attention in service establishments.
Nurturance	To give sympathy and help.	Working with employees to help them reach their goals.
Exhibition	To make an impression. To excite, amaze, fascinate, entertain, shock, intrigue, amuse, or entice others.	Wearing high-fashion clothing. Buying new products that are unconventional. Learning about new technology and products.
Cognizance	The need to explore, to ask questions, to seek knowledge.	Being opinion leaders. In-depth understanding of issues.
Exposition	The need to give information and explain, interpret, and lecture.	Consensus building.

Source: Jagdish Sheth and Banwari Mittel, "Customer Behavior: A Managerial Perspective," chap. 5 in H. A. Murray, *Explorations in Personality* (New York: Oxford, 1938).

who believed that people are not controlled by mechanical forces (the stimuli and reinforcement forces of behaviorism) or the unconscious instinctual impulses of psychoanalysis alone. Instead, Maslow focused on human potential, believing that humans strive to reach the highest level of their capabilities. Based on Maslow's theory, in order to reach this state of "self-actualization," one has to pass through four lower need levels.

The hierarchical theory is often illustrated as a pyramid, with the larger, lower levels representing the more basic needs and the upper point representing the need for self-actualization.[6] Each level of the pyramid is dependent on the previous level. For example, a person does not feel the second need level until the demands of the first need level have been satisfied. Here is a closer look at each of the need levels shown on the left side of Figure 2.3:

- *Biological/physiological needs.* These needs are biological and consist of the need for basic necessities: oxygen, food, water, and a relatively constant body temperature. These needs are the strongest because, if deprived of them, a person will die.

- *Security/safety needs.* Except in times of emergency or periods of disorganization in the social structure, adults do not display their security needs. After the terrorist attack on September 11, 2001, however, people around the world began purchasing more security-related products. Businesses also increased their security-related purchases.

- *Social (love, affection, and belonging) needs.* People need to escape feelings of loneliness and alienation. They need to give and receive love and affection, and they need a sense of belonging. Amiables, in particular, strive to build consensus in their organizations and meet these social needs.

- *Ego/esteem needs.* A person needs a stable, firmly based, high level of self-respect and respect from others in order to feel satisfied, self-confident, and valuable. If these needs are not met, the person feels inferior, weak, helpless, and worthless. Key decision-makers at high levels in organizations have healthy egos. You should make sure to show respect for their authority and position. Drivers, in particular, have a high need to be respected, while analyticals have a high need to be right.

FIGURE 2.3 Maslow's Hierarchy of Needs and Information

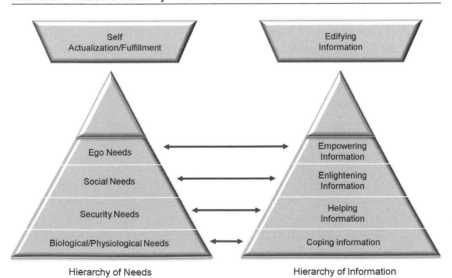

- *Self-actualization/fulfillment.* Maslow described self-actualization as an ongoing process. Self-actualizing people are involved in a cause outside of themselves (i.e., doing good for others). They are devoted to working in some calling or vocation. Many senior-level executives participate in charities as a way of giving back to the community. Their involvement in various nonprofit organizations helps them attain self-actualization and fulfillment.

Hierarchy of Information

Maslow's hierarchy of needs can be translated into a hierarchy of information needs for use in selling. In business, people at each level in the needs hierarchy seek information, from basic to more advanced, to help them deal with what is important to them. The right side of Figure 2.3 illustrates the hierarchy of information needs in more detail:

- *Coping information:* Information that is needed when an organization is sick, losing money, or facing a new competitive threat. In selling to organizations, you should appeal to this need by sharing relevant information with your prospects about how your product or service will help the organization survive by reducing operating costs and/or improving productivity.
- *Helping information:* Information on how to protect and defend profitability and/or market share. You, as a trusted advisor, can help your business prospects defend against their competitors.
- *Enlightening information:* Information on how to improve business performance. You can also enlighten your prospects about new tools and processes that will facilitate enhancements in the way they and their businesses perform.
- *Empowering information:* Information to enhance employee performance. Many business executives are concerned about improving employee productivity. Demonstrate how your solution (i.e., your product or service) will improve the way a prospect's employees perform.
- *Edifying information:* Information that provides special business support beyond your information about product performance. As a trusted advisor, you should constantly challenge yourself to help your prospects succeed in the area of community awareness. This re-

quires you to be creative. For example, you may arrange an event to be sponsored by a prospect, utilizing your product or service, and coordinate the donation of a portion of the proceeds from the event to a local charity. Such an approach would contribute to the prospect's public relations and facilitate the prospect's self-actualization.

Maslow's hierarchy of needs can be further applied to business customers, as Jagdish Sheth and Banwari Mittal illustrated in "Customer Behavior: A Managerial Perspective."[7] The authors applied the needs hierarchy on two levels: the business customer as an enterprise, and prospects/customers as individuals working in firms.

As an enterprise, business firms need, for their physical survival, resources such as money, employees, raw materials, and equipment. Banks and venture capitalists that supply cash, recruitment agencies that supply employees, and suppliers of raw materials and equipment all cater to the survival needs of the business enterprise, which are at the same level as the biological/physiological needs of the individual.

Security needs for business firms translate into insurance against loss of property and assets, and against liabilities that may arise in various business transactions. Indeed, safety and security are key concerns in government and business buying.

Social/belonging needs for business enterprises include the need for recognition by peer organizations and admission to formal or informal membership groups of other similar organizations. Being listed by *Fortune 500* or listed on the stock exchange and belonging to the Better Business Bureau are examples of the need to belong in business.

Esteem for a business enterprise comes partly from being recognized by various organizations and partly from a sense of accomplishment—for example, winning the Malcolm Baldrige National Quality Award, given by the President of the United States for performance excellence. In order to belong to certain groups and win certain awards, businesses need to tightly control quality in raw materials, train their employees well, reengineer services, and so on. Those are examples of how you can tailor your products and services to fit this psychological need.

Finally, business firms can achieve self-actualization by striving to become the ideal company. For example, 3M is known as the innovation company, Ben & Jerry's as the environmental company, Levi Strauss as the diversity company, and Benetton as the socially conscious company. You must learn how important these values are to your business customers in order to help your prospects achieve *their* goals. To be successful, you must think beyond just selling products; you need to relate your products to the buying organization's goals and create ways to help your customers' companies achieve self-actualization.

Today's salesperson must be adept at finding out what prospects want *and* why they want it. As demonstrated, in business-to-business selling, prospects buy for both business (e.g., increased market share and profitability) and personal (e.g., personal recognition and promotion) reasons. You need to sell to both! Tension—the gap between the current state and the desired state—is at the core of what motivates buyers to buy.

3 *Preparation*

By failing to prepare, you are preparing to fail.
—Benjamin Franklin

The Preparation Step

Are salespeople born or made? It certainly helps if you inherently possess the *natural talent*—the basic personality traits and aptitude for a profession in sales. Nevertheless, what separates the talented salesperson from the successful salesperson is preparation—always being in a state of readiness. George Washington Carver said it most aptly: "There is no short cut to achievement. Life requires thorough preparation—veneer isn't worth anything."[1]

This chapter begins the sequence in the *science* of selling. Its purpose is to explain how research should be conducted to properly prepare for a professional sales presentation. The preparation step involves finding out, as best as one can, who the prospects are, what they need, and why they need or want it. It will discuss the different types of information to be gathered and give tips for developing a high-impact sales presentation. Within the preparation stage, the professional salesperson prepares by first conducting research to secure information about the prospective customer—the organization and the people within an organization who have a high likelihood of buying. This step is typically called prospecting, and it is critical to the preapproach.

Finding prospects that can purchase is not as easy as it may sound. In sales of industrial products, too many sales calls are made to the wrong person. Alexander Graham Bell once said, "When one door closes, another opens; but we often look so long and so regretfully upon the closed door that we do not see the one which had opened for us."[2] So it is with prospecting. Customers appear and disappear. You need to have a systematic approach to prospecting in order to avoid calling on the wrong person. Here are some best practices for prospecting and tips for locating the most likely prospects in order to avoid making sales calls to prospects that are unlikely to buy the product.

Rudyard Kipling wrote some of the most quoted lines in English literature, including:

> I keep six honest serving men,
> They taught me all I know,
> Their names are what and where and when,
> And how, and why and who.
> —Rudyard Kipling, "The Elephant's Child" (1902)

There may be no better way to prepare for a sales presentation than to answer these six questions: who? what? why? how? where? and when?

Obtaining Knowledge—The Preapproach

The objective of the preapproach is to conduct an assessment of the customer's situation in order to improve your ability to match what the customer has in mind as a potential solution to her business problem. The pages that follow contain a framework for organizing the kind of knowledge that you need in order to build long-term relationships with customers. This framework includes the following knowledge areas: the customer, the sales organization, the competition, and the environment.

The Customer

Who are the people in the buying center/decision-making unit? *What* roles do they play? In *what* products are they interested, and *what* products have they bought before? *Why* do they want or need these products? *How* will the buying decision be made? *Where* will the decision be made, and *when* will it be made? Table 3.1 provides an extensive list of customer organizational knowledge areas.

Keep in mind Jag Sheth's comments in the Foreword of this book. Loyal clients believe that trusted advisors: (1) have the client's best interest in

TABLE 3.1 Areas of Customer Knowledge

- Key buying influencers, their respective roles, and how they make decisions

- How prospects and customers use or can use products/services

- Customer buying cycles

- Necessary activities to maintain relationships with customers

- Customers' technical evaluation criteria for all products/services

- Customers' growth plans

- Customers' organization, management structure, and lines of responsibility and authority

- Customers' preferred suppliers

- Other suppliers with whom customers talk

- Degree to which customers like to be kept up-to-date

- Customers' preferred communications channels for various sales and relationship-building activities

- What prospects generally are looking for regarding sales organization products/services

mind; (2) do everything possible to make the client successful; (3) make their clients look good; (4) are leaders in their respective fields; (5) adapt their experience to their client's circumstances; and (6) are open to feedback to improve performance.[3]

If an organization is a current customer, remember events can change the customer's situation and alter the value propositions that have been relevant to that customer. You can refer to past records for customer knowledge. New-customer knowledge, however, is also needed and might come in the form of newspaper or magazine articles about the customer organization, inquiries via email or the Internet, or information published by the customer, such as annual reports, newsletters, and webpages. You cannot be idle. Stay up-to-date on the customer's organization. The methods for obtaining such knowledge range from simply asking questions of customer personnel to more elaborate information-gathering techniques, such as customer satisfaction surveys. People are sharing lots of useful information online by way of social networks, such as LinkedIn, Facebook, and Twitter, to name a few. Social media encourages sharing and interaction, from product awareness to product discussions, from targeting potential customers to building and maintaining good business relationships.

If you have difficulty finding information about a specific prospect company, you can learn about the industry. At one time, American Telephone and Telegraph, Inc. (AT&T) maintained undersea cables owned jointly by AT&T, Canadian Bell, and several European telecom firms. A salesperson who was asked to visit a subsidiary of AT&T knew nothing about the subsidiary company but decided to learn about the industry. She located a book on undersea cables, written for junior high school students, that provided conversational knowledge of the subject—how the cables were laid and how they might be repaired. This basic knowledge allowed her to listen to the prospect, ask relevant questions, and propose a course of action. The prospect knew the salesperson was no expert in undersea cables but was impressed with the work ethic she had demonstrated in reading about the subject. The salesperson's efforts suggested the level of commitment that she would give to the prospect if he became a customer. Employing product knowledge in selling is not always this simple, but in this example, the salesperson had a choice: meet the prospect with no cable knowledge or spend a little time gaining some preliminary knowledge. The latter strategy may not always work, but the former strategy will never work.

Customer Personal Knowledge

You must never lose sight of the fact that no matter how large an organization is, its products and services are purchased by *people* who have their own wants and needs. Thus, information about the organization's people is quite important to you.

Professional selling is about communication between two or more people who are acting as seller and buyer. Communication improves as you and your buyers share more experiences. So, as simple as it may seem, the selling process is often made easier when you can ask about personal details (e.g., how a buyer's daughter is doing in school or whether a buyer's son has earned his black belt). Every individual has hot buttons, topics in which that individual is particularly interested. If you know what these topics are and use them skillfully, you can facilitate the selling process.

Many salespeople fail in the area of personal knowledge of customers because their interest is not sincere. You cannot simply mumble "How ya' doin?" and expect anything more than a polite reaction such as "Fine." You must know your buyers' interests; don't guess at such matters. Do your homework, update your information, and combine new data with previously learned information in order to broaden your knowledge of customers.

The Sales Organization

Often, you are the sales organization in the eyes of buyers. Therefore, you must be knowledgeable about your sales organization: its products and services, personnel, history, current status, and so on. Table 3.2 presents a detailed look at the sales organization knowledge areas required of you.

Most of the knowledge areas in Table 3.2 are self-explanatory, but a few words about personnel and history are necessary. Many customers expect you to be knowledgeable about the sales organization's personnel; for example, customers may ask: "Is Mr. Teepell still the vice president of sales in the Northeast region?" "When will Mr. Zehnder launch that new mobile application he's been talking about?" "Who will be the new manager in the local branch office?" Sometimes such questions are the stuff of idle conversation, and sometimes the customer is truly interested in the answers. In either case, you must be able to maintain your end of the conversation.

It is also important that you know the history of your organization. Such knowledge allows you to build rapport with veteran buyers who have been doing business with your sales company for many years. Nostalgia can be an icebreaker in many conversations. Historical knowledge also provides you with a stronger sense of belonging to the organization.

Product Prices

Prices are sensitive subjects for prospects and therefore a knowledge area of which you must be adept. They often represent the most difficult and worrisome aspects of sales organization knowledge for you. Although it is common to hear that customers buy based on value and not on price, it is often the price (as a determinant of value) that makes the difference in a sales presentation. Price is evaluated by prospects in relation to competitors' prices, quality, performance, product availability, delivery, and many other bases of comparison.

TABLE 3.2 Areas of Knowledge about the Sales Organization

Product

Personnel

History

Organizational Policies
- Raw Materials—quality, inspection processes, sources
- Labor—rate of pay, skill levels, working conditions
- Financing—stability of firm

Credit Terms

Production Methods

Service

Distribution
- Which channels
- Policy on exclusive dealerships
- Policies on selective distribution
- Protection provided by suppliers to channel members
- Price policies
- Price discounts
- Terms of sale
- Promotional programs
- Brand policy (private vs. name)

Communication Channels
- Internet
- Catalogs
- Personal
- Phone

Prices
- Competitiveness
- Entry—pricing strategy to make products attractive to prospects
- Lines—products available in a number of price categories

Rebates and Discounts
- Rebate availability
- Quantity discounts
- Seasonal discounts—to balance production and inventory
- Cash discounts
- Trade discounts—to channel members in return for services
- Trade-ins
- Advertising allowances—supplier helps channel members promote products/ services
- Push money—monetary incentives for pushing certain products/services
- Shipping costs

Delivery
- What?
- How?
- When?
- How often?
- What quantities?

Competitive Position
- Key differentiators

Sales Support

Sales Support Services

Sales support services relate to the service the selling organization makes available to customers in conjunction with the primary products and services it sells. Sales support often represents a way for you to augment the basic features and benefits of your primary product or service. For this reason, you must be knowledgeable about your organization's services. Sales support includes:

- Shipping and delivery
- Advertising programs
- Sales promotional programs
- Sales literature and catalogs
- Merchandising support
- Website support
- Credit provisions
- Financial services
- Design services
- Installation
- Instructions for use
- Employee training
- Technical inspection
- Maintenance and repair
- Consultation and evaluation
- Studies and recommendations

Support services can be a major value-added tool for you. Sales support can help in the sales of products and services, ensure their proper use, and create customer satisfaction. Customer service support is key in adding to the value of the product or service and in helping relationships with customers grow.

Product Knowledge

It goes without saying that product knowledge is a must. Product knowledge is the foundation upon which selling is built. Many prospects, however, feel that salespeople have inadequate product knowledge. Salespeople often know the features of their products but have difficulty presenting those features to prospects in the form of benefits that will solve customers' problems.

Prospects buy *solutions;* the product is incidental. Selling is value creation, not just product communication. You must see solutions within your product offerings that would be beneficial to your prospects. For example, a salesperson from a company selling a forklift capable of lifting a pallet that is 16 feet wide and 8 feet long, weighing 40,000 pounds, to a height of 14 feet, can present these features of the forklift to a prospect. This type of product knowledge is factual, technical, objective, and absolutely essential for sales success. However, this type of information also must be converted to product benefits during the salesperson's presentation. For example, the forklift minimizes the amount of time the prospect's trucks spend at the loading dock, which saves time, reduces costs, and increases the prospect's ability to make more deliveries. Do you see how the way the information is presented can make a difference?

The Competition

This chapter and the following ones will provide considerable insight into how important it is for you to know your competition. You must be up-to-date concerning the competitive position your organization holds in the marketplace, since it is only with knowledge of competitive offerings that you can evaluate the strengths and weaknesses of your own products in individual selling situations. For example, if you have a superior but little-known product in a market that is dominated by well-established brand names, you must present a message that demonstrates the merits of your product to customers. Perhaps being less known means you and your company will work harder for the customer. Alternatively, if your sales organization's competitive position is strong, you should capitalize on the "big company" resources your company can bring to the business relationship.

Knowledge about Competitive Products

You seldom pursue an unobstructed course to landing a customer order. Competitors get in the way with their product claims. In order to handle competitors' claims successfully, you must become almost as familiar with your competitors' products as with your own. This is another component of gathering knowledge about the competition.

In order to become well acquainted with competitors' products and their performance characteristics, you can examine the competitive products personally and observe how they perform. Another less direct but very productive method of gathering information about the competition is to study competitors' sales literature and advertisements. You should objectively analyze all competitive product claims that are reported by customers, who are usually quite willing to relay such claims. Customers often do this to challenge you to validate your message that your product is better than the competition's.

Regardless of the sources used to obtain information on competitive products, you are wise to analyze the characteristics of your competitors' products systematically and to record your findings in a CRM database. This helps in thinking about how to deal constructively with competitors' claims. Such a record can be similar in format to the features-benefits inventory in Table 3.3. Catalog the confirmable disadvantages of competitive products along with the offsetting benefits of your own product.

TABLE 3.3 Features-Benefits Inventory Form

Product: _____

Product Features	Customer Benefits	Customer Coding
1.	1a.	Customer 1
	1b.	Customer 2
	1c.	Customer 3
2.	2a.	Customer 4
3.	3a.	Customer 1
	3b.	Customer 4

As a caution, speaking negatively about a competitive product is never wise. Even if you think you have valid evidence of negative information about your competition, there is always a risk that the information is wrong. Therefore, you should sell the strengths of your products rather than your competitors' weaknesses.

The exclusive features of your company's product or service can give you a terrific advantage over the competition, which makes it easy for you to demonstrate how your product or service can help customers gain a benefit or avoid a loss. In this capacity, you enable customers to improve their situations and develop long-term relationships with them.

The Environment

The last piece required in the knowledge management framework is knowledge of the environment. The first environmental factor that comes to mind in selling is the competition-prospect interface. Obtaining knowledge about the competitive position is vital, but you must also realize that no product or service is completely unique. Competitors are attempting to provide similar offerings to satisfy prospects' wants and needs. Therefore, you must think of your products from the perspective of the wants or needs they will satisfy. For example, General Motors is not in the car and truck business; it is in the transportation business, competing against other car companies, mass transit, and producers of bicycles and walking shoes. Manufacturers of DVDs provide entertainment, competing against the theater, softball games, bowling, and many other activities. Brick sellers compete against lumber sellers. Credit unions compete with banks. You can easily lose sight of the competition-prospect interface if you think you are selling products instead of satisfying wants and needs.

The sales environment also includes a number of other factors that can lead to changing business conditions of which you need to be aware. These factors include government policies, existing and impending legislation, technology, the economic situation, regulatory agencies such as the Federal Trade Commission, the ecological impact products may have, and what is happening in the global marketplace. It is a challenge to stay up-to-date on all of this information. Hence the importance of knowledge management, customer relationship management, and the support of the sales organization in helping you manage and use knowledge to serve customers is emphasized. Table 3.4 contains a checklist of essential information you must know before meeting with customers.

Thus far, the focus has been on one-to-one selling and on the relationship between a buyer and a seller. The following section discusses selling to multiple people in an organization, which is typical of business-to-business selling.

TABLE 3.4 Essential Preapproach Background Information

Prospect as an individual	a. Name—spell it correctly!
	b. Age—older people like respect
	c. Education
	d. Residence
	e. Need for your product
	f. Ability to buy
	g. Authority to buy
	h. Facts about family
	i. Membership groups
	j. Best time to see individual
	k. Personal peculiarities
	l. Interests
	m. Personality/social style
Personnel of the company	a. Who owns the company
	b. Who has the final word on purchases
	c. Who else influences the business
Company operations	a. What it makes/sells
	b. What markets
	c. Product quality
	d. Plant capacity
	e. What parts are made/bought
	f. Type of machinery used to produce
	g. Raw materials—kind/source
	h. Seasonal factors
Buying practices of the company	a. Procedures of the purchasing department
	b. Few or many sources of supply
	c. Credit rating
	d. Quantity of purchase
	e. Satisfaction with supply sources
	f. Reciprocity agreements

Organizational Buying

Organizations do not buy, *people* do. In many organizations, teams of people do the buying. Therefore, you must focus your communications on the motivations, perceptions, and power of the individuals who make up the buying team.

In a buying team, more than one team member may be able to negate a transaction and a relationship. Even people who are lower in the organization, such as analysts, may have this capability if they express doubt about whether your proposal can meet the needs of the buying organization. Moreover, buying-team members can delay the completion of a sale by expressing a need to learn more, to gather more information, or to have more tests run. Therefore, you must have an in-depth understanding of the members of the buying team. You should add to your knowledge any information that helps you know the buying-team members better, and you should tailor your communications to the needs of each team member.

Table 3.5 presents a format that you can use to organize your knowledge of buying-team members. This chart includes the salesperson's assessment of what motivates the team members, how they view the salesperson and the sales organization, and whether they have the ability to negate or delay a sale. The next section shows how to expand this knowledge by identifying the various roles played by those in a buying center.

TABLE 3.5 Developing a Knowledge Base Related to the Buying Team

	Team Member	Title	Motivation	Perception	Role	Delay Power	Negate Power
1.							
2.							
3.							
4.							
5.							
6.							
7.							

Source: Adapted from B. P. Shapiro, *Sprint Sell to Close Sales Quickly* (Boston: Harvard Business School Publishing, 2001).

The Buying Center

You should identify all participants involved in a buying situation before making a call. Understanding the distinct roles that people in the buying process play helps you influence the buying decision. The following text discusses the five roles—users, influencers, deciders, buyers and gatekeepers—played by each member of the buying team.

Users

Users influence the buying decision by recognizing the need for a product and defining many of the product characteristics that will fulfill that need. The individuals who actually use the product often develop specifications for the product they desire. They may favor a particular salesperson because of a personal bias, or they may refuse to work with one company's products because of an earlier unfavorable opinion.

Influencers

Individuals in a variety of positions may directly or indirectly influence the buying decision. They may be major forces in determining purchasing criteria, or they may simply provide information to help the buying team evaluate alternative products. You should imagine the possible influences these people can have, and you should be ready to address their concerns. For example, technical personnel in a hospital laboratory may be important influencers if they have the opportunity to specify one product over another. In manufacturing organizations, engineers often influence the purchasing agent's choice of materials to be used in manufacturing new products. Product scheduling, research, design engineering, and management also may influence the buying process by emphasizing product characteristics they find desirable or by directing how a purchase is to be made. Financial officers, for example, may influence whether purchases are made on certain credit terms if they are concerned about cash flow.

Deciders

Deciders make the final decisions within the buying center. In many instances, the decider is the buyer, but the decider may be any one of the influencers in the purchase. For example, to save funds, a hospital financial officer may make the final decision on a product based upon the payment terms, but he may leave the purchasing details to the buyer. In other cases, the engineering or research and development people may make the final decision.

Buyers

Buyers actually make the physical purchase. Purchasing or procurement agents, as they are often called, set up the formal arrangements for the purchase and may make the final decision. Even though a purchasing manager or agent has the formal authority to select a sales company or vendor, that person may be limited in this decision by constraints from influencers and/or users. The power of the buyer varies with the situation surrounding the purchase. Purchases to satisfy old needs may be routine (e.g., a straight rebuy), and the buyer may have unlimited authority to establish product criteria and make final purchase decisions. However, when there is a new need that is very costly or technically complicated, the buyer's power to make the purchase decision may be constrained by the input of many influencers.

Gatekeepers

One other role that is important to you is that of the person who controls the flow of information in the organization, or the gatekeeper. Administrative assistants usually operate as gatekeepers. Purchasing agents also may play this role, but general management or technical personnel may actually hold the role.

The Buying Process Matrix

All the individuals discussed here—users, influencers, deciders, buyers, and gatekeepers—form a buying center, also known as a decision-making unit. The buying center can be examined in more detail by using the buying process matrix in Figure 3.1. You should identify the buying center for the appropriate cells in the buying process model, while remembering that the buying center changes with each cell in the matrix. In reordering company stationery, for instance, the buyer will ordinarily call the supplier that furnished the last order. However, if the administrative assistant (who is the gatekeeper and buyer in this example) decides that the company's image could be improved by a new look, the need is modified, and the influencers could be many.

FIGURE 3.1 The Buying Process Matrix

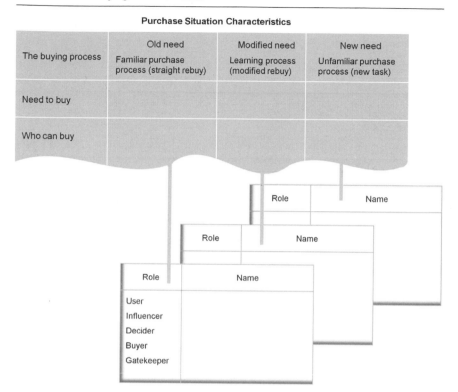

All organizational buyers are interested in the rational aspects of products and services that can lead to increases in sales and/or profitability, but all the individuals involved in buying do not rank all considerations equally. For example, some buyers are cost-conscious, while others are more concerned about product and service quality and uniformity. In order to capitalize on sales opportunities, you must be aware of the factors that motivate an organizational buyer to purchase, as well as the importance of each individual factor. Table 3.6. provides examples of buying criteria found in various company departments that may have individuals participating as part of the buying team.

Identifying the Prospect

As you begin identifying prospects, you will uncover many leads, also referred to as suspects. As you will see later in this chapter, good leads gener-

Table 3.6 Examples of Organizational Buyers' Criteria

Accounting Department

- Offers volume discounts
- Regularly meets quality specifications
- Is honest in dealing
- Answers all communications promptly
- Has competitive prices
- Handles product rejections fairly
- Provides needed information when requested (such as bids)

Manufacturing/Engineering Department

- Delivery when promised
- Provides products during times of shortages
- Regularly meets quality specifications
- Can deliver quickly in an emergency
- Is honest in dealing
- Allows credit for scrap or rework
- Has a low percentage of rejects

Production Control Department

- Can deliver quickly in an emergency
- Ships products when wanted (e.g., move up and/or push back deliveries if necessary)
- Regularly meets quality specifications
- Willing to cooperate in the face of unforeseen difficulties
- Helpful in emergency situations

Special Machinery Engineering Department

- Provides products during times of shortages
- Regularly meets quality specifications
- Has a low percentage of rejects
- Delivers when promised
- Is honest in dealing

Purchasing Department

- Regularly meets quality specifications
- Advised of potential trouble
- Is honest in dealing
- Provides products during times of shortages
- Willing to cooperate in the face of unforeseen difficulties
- Delivers when promised
- Provides needed information (such as bids) when requested

Tool Design Department

- Is honest in dealing
- Has technical ability and knowledge
- Handles product rejections fairly
- Allows credit for scrap or rework
- Invoices correctly
- Provides products during times of shortages
- Answers all communications properly

ally come from referrals, which can come from satisfied customers and clients. When you obtain a lead, you do not know if this suspect has a need, can afford to purchase your product or service, or has the authority to make a purchase decision.

Following are some ideas on building a prospect file. It is recommended that you select and try the techniques to learn objectively which methods will work for you.

Prospecting Techniques

Sources of prospects include sales managers, customers, the Internet and directories of all kinds, inquiries, trade shows, advertising, conventions, and the like. Many techniques can be used to define prospects, but it is more helpful to have a framework for thinking about such techniques than it is to list them all. Consequently, these prospecting techniques are grouped into three categories, and several of the most common techniques in each category are discussed. The three categories are: *internal sources of prospects, prospects found by intelligence and knowledge management, and prospects generated through specific actions.*

Identifying Prospects through Internal Sources

Many prospect sources can be found within your own organization, which is probably the first place you should look for prospects. Major internal sources include the following.

1. *Sales records.* You can return to the same customers repeatedly. Although this might leave many new prospects uncalled on, previous customers often buy again. Selling to former customers may sound like a simple, and perhaps obvious, idea, but it is surprising how many salespeople overlook it and do not systematically prospect their past accounts. Ideally, you should maintain a tickler file, a calendar-based filing system that reminds you when customers might be ready to reorder staple supplies, carry out a planned plant expansion, and so forth. Even when you have no records on previous customers other than their names, you are well advised to check periodically with those customers, and certainly when taking over new territories you

should carefully review the sales records. Again, CRM systems can help sales organizations with important record-keeping tasks, and they are invaluable when it comes to mining customer data (e.g., past purchases) for sales opportunities.

2. *Organizational promotional activities.* In addition to having a sales force, most organizations promote their products and services through various media, such as in advertising and at trade shows where they display their wares. Ideally, this promotional activity is coordinated with personal selling so that you can follow up on inquiries from potential customers. Advertisements encourage suspects to send for free brochures that provide information about products and services, and postage-free return cards are often included in the brochures so recipients can send for additional information. In advertising, approximately one out of every ten leads will yield a sale. You also should not overlook the annual reports produced by publicly traded companies; these reports are actually advertisements for the companies and usually contain valuable information that can be used in prospecting.

3. *Referrals.* Organizational members who are not salespeople often come into contact with potential customers. Repair and service personnel probably have the best chance to identify prospects by the referral method. Salespeople for one product line may uncover prospects for another of the organization's products. And all organizational members have professional and even social contacts through which they might identify suspects. Everyone in the organization should be encouraged to refer potential customers to you.

4. *Inquiries.* Many firms receive direct inquiries about products or services from customers. Buyers are always seeking lower costs and additional supply sources. Sales organizations can solicit inquiries through trade shows, conventions, advertising, and inquiry-reply cards. In addition, the Internet is a great tool for lead generation. A growing number of inquiries are made via company websites. Potential customers visit websites for general information, and some websites trigger email to the salespeople who cover the potential customers' geographic territories so the salespeople can follow up on these leads.

Identifying Prospects through Market Intelligence

In this second category of prospecting techniques, "intelligence" is used in the military sense: the collection and analysis of environmental information. Like the spy, the salesperson has a great deal of information available for the asking; it needs only to be captured and evaluated. Typical sources of intelligence include the following:

1. *Lists.* We are a society of list-makers. Every individual's name appears on many lists: the telephone directory, newspaper and magazine subscriber lists, lists of holders of credit cards, membership lists (e.g., Kiwanis or the Rotary Club), church rosters, and lists of students and organizational employees. A list of possible lists would be virtually endless. Such lists are valuable prospecting tools. A telephone directory, for example, lists dentists who must buy office equipment, building contractors who need plumbing fixtures, and so on.

2. *Crisscross directory.* A crisscross directory, also called a reverse telephone directory, lists the names and telephone numbers of people with common characteristics—for example, everyone living on a given street and served by the same telephone exchange, or everyone with two or more children. Similarly, college alumni organizations have databases of their graduates. Crisscross directories, which are available in print and online, can be used to identify people who are potential customers.

3. *News media.* One of the cheapest, most accessible, and up-to-date sources of prospects is the newspaper. Financial services salespeople, for example, take note of wedding and birth announcements, graduation announcements, and the like. Building supply salespeople watch for announcements of new shopping centers and building permits, classified ads for workers, and reports of fires and other catastrophes that destroy buildings. The society page is of interest to salespeople of such items as home furnishings, clothing, and jewelry. Another excellent source is trade publications; most industries have publications that carry the news in that particular industry. Specialized insider's newsletters attempt to provide information to their subscribers before it appears in the news media. All of these media are potential sources of prospects for the alert and agile salesperson.

You should subscribe to the trade journals in your industry, since in addition to providing needed information about your respective industries, these journals are a great source of leads.

4. *Government sources.* Government permits or licenses are required for many activities today—building and construction, utility connections, office openings by doctors and lawyers, purchases of automobiles and guns, decisions to marry or divorce, and new business ventures. Information about permits and licenses is compiled by government offices and is often available for public inspection. Sometimes there is a nominal fee for obtaining such information, but often these records are available for inspection without a charge. A little thinking on a salesperson's part will suggest an appropriate governmental record for obtaining leads in selling almost any product. For example, plumbing and heating contractors are interested in new building permits, automobile insurance agents are interested in new car registrations, and salespeople of bar supplies are interested in new liquor licenses. The list goes on. For general background information, the U.S. Census Bureau is a great source of information.[4]

5. *Observation.* Many good prospects can be found simply by keeping your eyes open. Real estate professionals, for example, cruise along streets looking for houses with "for sale by owner" signs, empty buildings, new "for lease" signs, and so on. Representatives of paint companies look for rusty, chipped building surfaces. Salespeople for printing companies look for smudged or blurred halftones in printed documents. All of these observations can lead you to prospects.

6. *Electronic databases.* Most sales organizations have automated their prospect lists and now keep them in electronic databases. There are also many online databases available to create prospecting lists for lead generation.

7. *SIC numbers.* The Standard Industrial Classification (SIC) system, designed by the U.S. Department of Commerce, assigns a numeric classification to each area of business. This system allows you to determine what products a particular company may purchase, as well as how much it buys. The primary drawback of the SIC system is that firms are classified only according to their principal products, so it may be more difficult to find out about other products produced by firms that specialize in more than one.

8. *NAICS numbers.* The North American Industry Classification System (NAICS) is the standard used by federal statistical agencies in classifying business establishments for the purpose of collecting, analyzing, and publishing statistical data related to the U.S. business economy. NAICS was developed under the auspices of the Office of Management and Budget (OMB), and was adopted in 1997 to replace the Standard Industrial Classification (SIC) system. Several data sets are still available with SIC-based data. Both SIC and NAICS classify establishments by their primary type of activity.

Identifying Prospects by Specific Actions

The third category of prospecting techniques is identifying prospects by specific actions. Although internal sources and market intelligence will uncover a number of prospects, most successful salespeople also attempt to generate leads by taking action on their own. For example, major account executives who deal with top executives often use a letter with a follow-up telephone call as a key prospecting approach. Organizations that sell to other organizations also use this approach because it supplies the prospect with information and allows the salesperson to follow up with decision-makers. Such salespeople and companies create lists of potential customers using a variety of methods. Here are some examples:

1. *Referrals.* Obtaining referrals is a time-honored custom. Ask your customers to supply the names of others who might also desire the product. Obviously, this method puts a premium on satisfying existing customers in hopes that they will endorse your sales organization. The endless-chain approach is one referral method in which you ask for names of additional prospects after each sales call. Naturally, those who have just bought your product are enthusiastic and generally are very willing to give you names of their friends and acquaintances.

   Another referral method is the center-of-influence approach. "Centers of influence" are opinion leaders—people in your territory who are influential. Church ministers, coaches, and professors, for example, can be centers of influence. If you can identify such opinion leaders in a particular territory and convince them of the value of your products, they can be sources for a number of good prospects.

There are many ways to obtain current customers' cooperation in providing referrals. First, you can mention to a current customer the names of a prospect or two that he knows and ask the customer to introduce you to them. He may be willing to write or even call them to set up a meeting. Another way to gain introductions from current customers is to distribute a supply of introductory cards on which customers can simply fill in the names of prospects. You can also carry a supply of postcards on which space is provided to list three or four new suspects; these cards can be left with customers in case they think of new suspects later. Emailed introductions have become more popular. Be sure to ask for them.

2. *Cold calls (cold canvassing).* Probably the bane of most salespeople's existence is the no-advance-preparation sales presentation to a total stranger. This situation is described by the term cold calling, also known as *cold canvassing.* The idea behind the cold call is that if you make enough contacts you will, by the law of averages, encounter some people who are prospects for your products. Cold canvassing for prospects is more likely to lead to frustration than to the identification of bona fide prospects. Nevertheless, most sales managers encourage their sales representatives to try cold calling, at least by telephone, when other prospecting methods have failed.

   Cold calling is best used only for certain types of products and services that are purchased by a large number of people. Vacuum cleaners, Girl Scout cookies, and cosmetics are representative products. For many other products and services, cold calls are very inefficient. You should always check local and state laws before using cold calling. Many U.S. states have enacted "Do Not Call" lists, allowing people to add their telephone number to a list that telemarketers are not permitted to contact. It is similar to the National Do Not Call List, which is managed and enforced by the FTC.

3. *Networking.* Four guidelines are suggested for salespeople who use networking to develop prospects: (1) meet as many people as you can, and make sure you tell the people you meet what you do; (2) always have business cards ready to distribute; (3) do not conduct business while networking, but set up future appointments for that; and (4) follow up on all contacts that seem as though they could be productive.

4. *Incentives.* You should express sincere appreciation for leads. You will have to use your own ingenuity and good judgment in selecting appropriate rewards for those who provide you with leads, but finding out what other successful salespeople in the area are doing will help.

5. *Other sales professionals.* You know other salespeople who work in noncompeting fields. They may be able to suggest prospects, since they understand how to identify prospects and can pass on valuable leads from their own territories, friends, and customers.

6. *Trade shows.* These shows represent an important element in the industrial marketer's promotional efforts. Trade shows are held for three reasons: (1) to allow customers and prospects to obtain information about products and services; (2) to provide participating companies with a forum in which to offer their products to prospective customers; and (3) to serve as excellent lead generators for salespeople. People who attend trade shows are there to learn about products, and industrial salespeople and other booth representatives are there to explain and demonstrate these products. Salespeople who work in booths at trade shows can collect intelligence on those visiting their booths and can follow up with the participants who show interest. In a sense, this form of prospecting is similar to the situation of the retail salesperson—the customer seeks out the salesperson, rather than the salesperson locating the customer.

   Often, conventions and trade shows attract thousands of people who are looking for the newest and best methods to help stimulate the growth of their businesses. Many firms do very little buying until they have visited such shows and have seen what new things are on the market. Trade shows give their buyers a chance to learn about what is available—to discover new products and to explore the advantages of specific types of products. An exhibitor at a trade show should have a registration book, referral cards, or some other method of getting the names and email addresses of prospects attending the show. Booth representatives should provide you with the names of the prospects who are located in your respective sales territories. You should give such prospects your immediate attention.

7. *Educational forums.* Some industries, like the pharmaceutical industry, host educational seminars that attract potential customers.

8. *Social media.* Start adding value regularly on Facebook, Twitter,

LinkedIn, or whatever social media platform you choose by becoming a content provider—an expert on a particular topic that might interest your prospects. Add links to connect with you on your email signature and all other electronic communications. Find out where your target market congregates on social media and join them.

Qualifying the Prospect

The qualification step in the prospecting stage is as important as the identification step, but its focus is different. Whereas the identification or search step focuses on creatively identifying possible prospects, the qualification step involves screening those prospects so that time is not wasted on those who cannot be converted to clients.

Lead qualification (prospect qualification) involves ascertaining such things as the prospect's budget, purchasing time frame, market position, and existing supplier situation, as well as the key people involved in the buying process. Salespeople must be careful not to approach lead qualification haphazardly. They must determine *who* in the sales organization is responsible for obtaining *what* information about the prospect, in *what* form the information is to be presented, and *when* that information must be assembled for use by the salesperson. Otherwise, the salesperson will be relegated to searching for suspects.

MAD Customers

Qualification involves assessing the prospect in terms of the sales organization's criteria to determine whether the prospect has one or more of the prerequisites that show the suspect is a realistic prospect: *money, authority,* and *desire* (hence the term *MAD customers*).

Money to Buy
The ability to buy a product is measured in terms of money or buying power. Three basic components of buying power can be distinguished: income, assets, and credit worthiness. In business-to-business (B2B) selling, you should be sure to review the company's financial standing (e.g., annual report) to determine whether the company has the financial resources

to purchase your product or service. You should also remember that you are selling *value;* if you can show that your product or service will save the company money (even more than time) in relation to the investment, you can make the sale.

Authority to Buy

Authority is the *legal* ability to buy and the power to consummate an exchange transaction. In many organizational situations, authority to buy can be difficult to determine. The lease or purchase of a new fleet of automobiles can involve a number of organizational personnel. You cannot afford to waste time and energy making presentations to people who do not have the authority to buy. Therefore, you should make sure to confirm, once you have met a prospect, whether the person with whom you are dealing has that authority.

Desire to Buy

The desire component is clearly a necessity for a prospective customer. The prospect must want the product. Personal selling and other marketing efforts can stimulate demand by both influencing and persuading people, but no selling or marketing effort, no matter how sophisticated or intense, can make people buy things they do not want. Remember, without desire, a prospect is not a qualified prospective customer.

Time and organizational resources will be wasted if you proceed to the later steps of the selling process with individuals who are not qualified.

In summary, the purpose of this chapter is not to catalog all prospecting methods, but rather to illustrate the many ways in which you can search for prospective customers. You should devote time and effort to the search and qualification phases during the prospecting stage of the selling process. Some companies are very creative in the ways they target specific potential customers. The key word is creativity. You must be resourceful. You must always be alert for and open to potential users of your products. Preparation is an essential part of being agile.

4   *Attention*

When you do the common things in life in an uncommon way, you will command the attention of the world.

—George Washington Carver

The Attention Step

Everyone has seen, and some have experienced, the reaction of soldiers when a drill sergeant issues the command, "Attention!" The soldiers become fixated on what the drill sergeant will say or do next. For you, gaining customers' attention is much more challenging. The power of rank does not exist in selling situations; however, the power of expertise does. The purpose of this chapter is to demonstrate how the knowledge gained in the preparation step is used to get prospects' attention and secure an appointment to present your value proposition.

Expertise is needed to address questions such as the following:

- How can you get a prospect to pay attention to what you are saying?
- If you and a prospect are not on the same thought track, how can there be a meeting of minds?
- How can you be sure you are on the same wavelength with prospects?
- Just because you meet a prospect, does that mean the prospect is necessarily ready to talk about what you want to talk about?
- How can you make prospects want to listen?
- What might prove to be your best attention-getter?
- How do you plan to get a prospect's immediate and favorable attention?

These challenges are why earning a prospect's attention is crucial. When prospects see you for the first time, they form a first impression—good or bad—that will last in their minds. Your looks (neatness, cleanliness, taste in clothes), actions (poise, confidence, assurance, courtesy), and manner of speaking (relaxed, clear, concise, modulated voice, enunciation, enthusiasm) can create a good impression in prospects' minds and influence them to let you continue with your sales presentation. A great way to make a positive first impression is to show the prospect that the spotlight is on them—to show that you are centered on the prospect's needs and wants.

Your first impression of a prospect provides a starting point for probing customer needs and for adapting to those needs. As a result, your effectiveness in an initial sales encounter is associated, at least in part, with the accuracy of *your* first impression of the prospect. You must know something about the prospect's needs and wants before you reach the attention stage, and you must use your knowledge obtained in the preparation stage to gain attention. Avoid letting personal first impressions interfere with your preparation.

It is *what* you say and *how* you say it that is most critical to engaging prospects. The objective of this chapter is to help you develop a thought process that will enable you to secure appointments under the right conditions and with a favorable attitude. People are seldom interested in a salesperson personally the first time they meet, but they can be very interested in what a salesperson says or does if it is related to what they want or need.

Open and honest communication, even early in the relationship-building process, is critical to the continuance of that process and to positioning yourself as a trusted advisor. Show that you are sincerely interested in the prospect's situation. Be well enough prepared to show a genuine interest in the prospect and the prospect's business. Prospects who develop trust in you are more likely to want to continue along the relationship path.

There is no second chance to make a first impression, but you will have many chances to build on a positive impression. You will enhance your ability to make a good first impression by listening. Offer positive responses like, "That's interesting," or "Tell me more about that." If the prospect is conversational, statements like these help create dialogue. Even after opening clear lines of communication and getting the attention of the prospect, you are faced with the challenge of *keeping* that person's attention.

You have only seconds to win or lose a prospect's attention. But once you get it, you must continue to earn it in 60-second increments, constantly doing or saying something to keep the prospect engaged. Using the prospect's name occasionally can be helpful; it makes your conversation more personal. "Marcus, I like that idea." Such a statement shows you have been listening. Again, just because you have the prospect's attention at one moment does not automatically mean that you can hold it. Most people have had the experience of talking with someone, maybe for several minutes, and suddenly being asked, "Who did you say you were with?" or "What did you say your name was?" or "How much did you say this costs?" At this point, you have finally gotten the prospect's attention. Although you had been talking all along, the prospect had not been really listening until you hit upon something that attracted his immediate attention.

Now that the importance and purpose of the attention step have been covered, the next section emphasizes three important components of the attention phase: *getting the appointment, making a positive first impression, and approaching the customer.*

Getting the Appointment

The first imperative of the attention stage is being able to present your value proposition to a prospect. This often requires getting an appointment. Some prospects are easy to see and like to talk. Some prospects are anxious to see representatives of prestigious firms. And some salespeople have such personal charm that they can get in to see almost anyone at any time.

Other salespeople, however, are not so fortunate. A prospect owes you neither time nor attention. That is why you should try to schedule appointments in advance. Appointments allow prospects to see you at their convenience and to prepare for such meetings if necessary. From your point of view, appointments are efficient. They save you travel time when prospects will not be available, and they often minimize the amount of time that you spend waiting to see prospects.

In order to talk to the right person, you may encounter and must cooperate with a prospect's gatekeepers and influencers. Administrative assistants generally operate as gatekeepers. One of the administrative assistant's tasks may be to screen calls in order to save the boss time. Consequently, you must convince the administrative assistant that the boss will want to hear what you have to say. If the administrative assistant is convinced, you can see the prospect. The term *gatekeepers* is used to describe such influencers because they control whether or not you get to see the decider.

The cardinal rule in getting an appointment is to remember that gate-keepers are people, too. Treat them accordingly. Experienced gatekeepers in office situations offer the following advice to salespeople like you:

1. Treat and respect me as a person rather than as part of the furniture. At least say hello, and possibly add a pleasantry or two.
2. Do not assume that you are the most important thing at the moment. Do not interrupt my telephone conversation or expect me to drop everything to usher you right in to see the boss.
3. Hand me your business card and say your name clearly.
4. Be patient. Some delays are unavoidable, and you can use the time productively.
5. Be friendly, but do not get too personal. Do not ask me for confidential information about my organization, my boss, or myself.
6. Do not tell me your troubles, particularly your gripes against my organization or yours.

In short, you may not even see a prospect at all if you do not treat the gate-keeper well.

An appointment is also likely to improve your effectiveness. By making appointments, you may find yourself seeing the people who really have the authority to buy, not necessarily the people with whom you originally thought you needed to talk. Appointments help you present an image of yourself as busy and organized, not as someone who has time to simply drop in for a chat. At the heart of the appointment issue is the potential dollar value of the sale, in the short run, or the projected value of an account in the longer term. Larger potential sales revenue accounts require more time and more depth of presentation, and thus fewer appointments. Smaller accounts are more abundant, but also require more calls and therefore more appointments.

If prospects are too easy to see, chances are they will not do you much good; they are probably so easy to get to because their authority is limited. Your goal is to call on the highest-ranking official in the company, and this person is likely to be very busy and difficult to see. Your primary objective, though, is to get to see the right prospect—the one who stands to benefit from purchasing and who has the authority to buy. You can be far more successful in qualifying prospects through letters and telephone calls than through personal visits, as these allow you to determine more quickly whether the person being contacted is the right person and whether she has any interest in your product.

There are many ways to contact prospects, but some of the more commonly used methods include telephone calls, in-person calls, letters through mail or email, and third-party introductions.

Telephone Calls

Perhaps the most frequently used method of securing an appointment is simply to telephone the prospect and ask for one (cold-calling). But before you make such a call, you must prepare for it. The objective is to secure an appointment, not to make your sales presentation. So you must talk in terms of the prospect's interests. By leading with a benefit, you can convince a prospect that seeing you would be worthwhile. An example of this approach is:

> Hello, Mr. Jeffrey. This is Paul Christie of General Manufacturing Company. We have a new jigsaw attachment that can help you double your production [benefit]. Over a short period of time, it can help you reduce your operating costs by one-third [benefit]. I would like fifteen minutes of your time to share with you how we can help improve your company's profitability. When may I drop in and show it to you?

Notice that in telephoning for an appointment, you should first state who is calling, whom you represent, what you are selling, and how the product will benefit the prospect, and then ask for the appointment. Also notice that the request for the appointment begins with an open-ended question: "When?" This question cannot be answered with a "yes" or "no." In contrast, a question such as, "May I drop in and show it to you?" invites the prospect to say "no." It also does not offer a compelling reason for the prospect to say "yes." You should always use open-ended questions and mention a reason (benefit) for wanting to see the prospect.

You may prefer to provide less information during an introductory phone call. You may feel comfortable stressing only the benefit of meeting with the prospect. In this way, you can gain more curiosity about your visit. So another way of saying what Paul said would be: "Mr. Jeffrey, my company has developed a new method for performing cutting operations, one that can double your production [benefit] and, over a short period of time, reduce your operational cost by one-third [benefit]. I would like to share with you how we can help improve your company's profitability. When is the best time for us to get together?" At this point, you are just selling the appointment, not the product or service, so the conversation should be brief.

No matter which approach is used, most prospects appreciate the consideration you show by phoning first. They will reciprocate by showing interest in the product. Approaching a prospect by telephone indicates that you do not want to waste either the prospect's or your time.

In-Person Calls

An in-person call, or cold calling, can be used to set up appointments for a later time. This is an excellent way to use an extra 15–20 minutes between appointments. You can visit other floors of the building in which you have an appointment, identifying likely prospects and asking for appointments with them. Your goal in making a cold call is to meet with the prospect face-to-face. If the prospect gives you access, you can proceed with your business. Keep in mind, however, that few prospects are willing to let you in without an appointment.

Letters

Writing letters is useful in initiating contacts with prospects. The usual approach is to send a letter briefly outlining the sales proposal and asking for an appointment to explain it fully. You can include a return postcard or email address, but don't count on the prospect replying voluntarily. You must indicate that you will follow up your letter or email in a defined time frame—for example, "I'll call next week to set an appointment with you." Sending a card or letter indicating when you will be in town is also a common practice. In many cases it is just as suitable to send an email. However, when selling to VITO, writing a formal letter is more appropriate. Table 4.1 provides information about how to secure appointments with VITO—the "very important top officer."

TABLE 4.1 Letters to VITO

Who (or What) Is a VITO?

VITO stands for "very important top officer" and refers to the one person in an organization with the ultimate decision-making power. Anthony Parinello's book *Selling to VITO* explains strategies professional salespeople can use to sell effectively to these top decision-makers.

How to Deal with VITOs

VITOs hate typical salespeople—the ones who talk a good game and focus solely on making a buck. VITOs avoid them like the plague. However, VITOs love getting calls from other professional businesspeople who can share news and views that are in the VITOs' best interests. Parinello admonishes salespeople to assume "equal business stature" when dealing with a VITO, which means understanding the VITO's situation and providing solutions to the VITO's problems.

Writing Letters to VITOs

When writing a letter to a VITO, a salesperson has less than eight seconds to capture the VITO's attention. Therefore, the salesperson should construct a headline statement that:

- Is 30 words or less
- Establishes the salesperson's credibility and equal business stature
- Addresses the VITO directly
- References a credible source to bolster the salesperson's case

In these statements, the salesperson should use power-packed words such as *guarantee, discover, benefit, value, advantage, proven results, quality, progress, growth, safe,* and *genuine.*

Source: Adapted from Anthony Parinello, *Selling to VITO: The Very Important Top Officer* (2nd ed.; Holbrook, Mass.: Adams Media, 1999).

Email Etiquette

Often a letter can be sent in the form of email, but the email must be professional and use the proper etiquette. It is important to follow email etiquette rules for the following three reasons:

1. *Professionalism.* By using proper language, you convey a professional image.
2. *Efficiency.* Emails that get to the point are much more effective than poorly worded emails.
3. *Protection from liability.* Your awareness of email risks will protect your company from costly lawsuits.

There are many etiquette guides and many different etiquette rules for email. Some rules differ according to the nature of the business and the corporate culture. Table 4.2 lists the most important email etiquette rules that apply to nearly all companies. Be careful when you send emails or letters not to close your communication with statements such as, "I'd like to visit with you to introduce myself and my company's products to you." Let's take a look at what this seemingly innocuous statement does not say. First, it does not communicate value in any way. Second, it offers no evidence that you can solve the prospect's problems. Third, it does not differentiate you, your product, or your company from competitors. As with phone calls, think value in your introductions and design them to get attention.

TABLE 4.2 Email Etiquette Tips

• Be concise and to the point	• Make it personal
• Answer swiftly	• Avoid using URGENT and IMPORTANT
• Use proper structure and layout	• Avoid long sentences
• Be careful with formatting	• Do not request delivery and read receipts
• Do not overuse the high-priority option	• Use meaningful terms for "subject"
• Do not write in CAPITALS	• Keep your language gender-neutral
• Do not leave out the message thread	• Do not reply to spam
• Add disclaimers to your emails	• Use cc: field sparingly
• Read the email before you send it	• Use templates for frequently used responses
• Do not overuse "reply to all"	• Use care with rich text and HTML messages
• Do not ask to recall a message	• Do not attach unnecessary files
• Use care with abbreviations and emoticons	• Do not forward virus hoaxes and chain letters
• Do not use email to discuss confidential information	• Use proper spelling, grammar, and punctuation
• Use active instead of passive sentence structure	• Answer all questions and preempt further questions
• Do not copy a message or attachment without permission	• For mass mailings, use the bcc: field or do a mail merge
• Do not send or forward emails containing libelous, defamatory, offensive, racist, or obscene remarks	

Third-Party Introductions

Third-party introductions are another way to get appointments with prospects. You can ask a satisfied customer not only to supply names of prospects but also to write a note introducing you to those prospects. The back of your business card can be used for this purpose. Third parties are particularly effective in business-to-business (B2B) situations, where more than one individual is involved in the buying situation. Here, you should seek initial contact with the highest-ranking individual in the buying center. It is easier to get an appointment with others, like the purchasing agent or shop foreman, if you can truthfully say that the vice president for finance suggested that you talk with them.

In many cases, getting an appointment is a selling situation in itself, so you should treat it as such. You should prepare carefully for it, just as you would do for the sales presentation. You should approach getting the appointment from the buyer's point of view and should ask for one in a positive, decisive, and courteous manner.

The First Impression

In many—perhaps most—selling situations, there is little difference between the products and services offered by different companies. So you personally often make the difference in whether or not a prospect buys. Therefore, you should be conscious of the communication signals you are sending.

Communication signals can be visual, vocal, verbal, or nonverbal. They are an important part of the first impression that you create in your introductions to prospects. When you meet someone in person, most of their first impression is based on nonverbal cues—your appearance, your body language, your perceived confidence. Over the phone, your tone of voice is mostly responsible for the first impression you create. If contacting a prospect by letter, pay attention to grammar, spelling, and style in order to make sure that your correspondence communicates professionalism. If you expect professional results, you must be thoroughly professional in all of your actions.

Appearance

How can you invite prospects to have confidence in you? One way is by presenting a pleasant and professional appearance. An old saying claims that "a picture is worth a thousand words." If this is so, what picture do you present as you walk through a prospect's office door? You must be visually appealing. Many prospects will judge you by your appearance, and their decision to buy or not buy can be made before you ever say a word.

To create the idea in a prospect's mind that she is being offered the best and latest professional advice available, you cannot afford to present yourself in any light other than your best. A prospect who sees a poorly dressed or poorly groomed sales representative is likely to be thinking, "If this person is this careless about his own appearance, he is probably too careless to look after my business!"

In preparing to meet a prospect, you need to dress appropriately. In general, you should dress like your prospects. However, you should always err on the side of conservatism. You should dress appropriately for the industry in which you are selling and particularly for the individual prospect.

Lombardi Time

The great Hall of Fame football coach of the Green Bay Packers, Vince Lombardi, developed a strategy that he recommended to his coaches and players. This strategy, which came to be known as "Lombardi time," embodies a valuable habit that is even more appropriate to you than to football players. Lombardi time states, "Show up for every important business meeting fifteen minutes ahead of the scheduled meeting time." The idea is that by showing up early for meetings, you can use the extra time to catch your breath, collect your thoughts, and rehearse what you want to accomplish in the meeting and how to go about it. This rule should be applied to all of your sales appointments and meetings and can be a key part of making a good first impression.

Sales Call Anxiety

You might be thinking, "I have an appointment. I made a good first impression. Now I am ready to approach the customer." You might also be wondering, "I made a good impression, so why am I feeling so anxious?" A prospect's first impressions can change based on reactions to such things as your sales company's website or promotional materials, something a competitor has said, or something another member of the prospect's buying center has said. You may not know the prospect's impressions have changed until you actually visit him. Much time may have elapsed between setting the appointment and the actual visit. The prospect may have obtained additional information about what you are offering.

Sales call anxiety (SCA) is an irrepressible fear of being negatively evaluated and rejected by a customer. The fear is accompanied by urges to avoid contact with customers or, when contact is made, to refrain from interacting effectively and asking for a commitment. Sales call anxiety can be exhibited in four different ways: negative self-evaluations, negative evaluations from customers, awareness of physiological symptoms (e.g., queasy stomach, shaky voice, blushing), and protective actions (e.g., avoiding eye contact, fiddling with hands, shunning self-disclosures). These feelings and actions can negatively influence your performance.[1] Table 4.3 provides suggestions for addressing SCA.

Courtesy and Common Sense

When first approaching a prospect, your opening statement, question, or action can identify you in his mind as either a time-waster or a professional salesperson. This presents you with an opportunity to use your imaginative abilities to see yourself as another person and to practice the golden rule—to do unto others as you would have them do unto you. What does the prospect want from you? You should try to imagine what you would want from a sales representative if you were suddenly to change places with the prospect.

Although the following guidelines for approaching the customer may seem elementary, experience shows that they are critically important and often overlooked. You should always remember that you are the prospect's guest and should:

1. Never sit down until invited to do so. You should ask for permission to sit.
2. Never clutter the prospect's desk with papers, a computer, a briefcase,

TABLE 4.3 Addressing Sales Call Anxiety

SCA Component	Approach
Negative self-evaluations	*Disconnect from negative thoughts.* • Focus on cues that reflect positive information and avoid cues that normally trigger overwhelming fears, which tend to occupy your memory. • Understand your self-worth.
Negative evaluations from customers	*Reduce approval seeking.* • Emphasize the matching of customer needs to your offerings and the matching of the sales strategy and specific appeals to the customer type. • Focus more on customer and product knowledge than on approval seeking and the need to belong.
Awareness of physiological symptoms	*Relax.* • Excessive focus on shaky hands, sweating, a quiver in the voice, or an upset stomach can aggravate social anxiety and interfere with interpersonal communication. • Concentrate on relaxing during a sales interaction. Take deep breaths before the sales call. • Engage in sports or recreation outside work to promote relaxation and renewal.
Protective actions	*Use self-regulatory tactics.* • Protective actions such as avoiding eye contact, speaking quickly, avoiding self-disclosures, and withdrawing prematurely in an effort to escape embarrassment can break down trust and lead customers to question the salesperson's competence. • Even before salespeople engage with customers, protective actions such as putting off calling a customer and other forms of procrastination, refusing to answer a telephone call from a customer, or planning to avoid certain topics in an anticipated exchange can lead to lost sales. • You can develop self-regulatory tactics to reduce anxiety, for example, using a script when customers raise questions or objections or when you feel an urge to avoid encounters or avoid discussing issues during an exchange. • To deal with a setback that occurs when a customer asks a product-related question to which you have no answer, respond by saying something like, "I cannot answer your question fully now, but I will call you back this afternoon after I investigate our policies more completely."

Source: Adapted from William Verbeke and Richard P. Bagozzi, "Sales Call Anxiety: Exploring What It Means When Fear Rules a Sales Encounter," *Journal of Marketing,* 64 (July, 2000): 88–101.

or other materials without asking for permission to place the materials on the desk.

3. Watch your tone of voice. Most prospects prefer listening to a calm, lower-pitched voice.
4. Always be courteous but not overly friendly or pushy.
5. Never be presumptuous. You should be cautious about calling prospects by their first names. You should address prospects formally (e.g., Mr., Mrs., Ms., Dr.) until the prospect invites you to use their first name.
6. Concentrate on making eye contact when meeting a prospect. Most prospects subscribe to the cliché, "Never trust a person who can't look you in the eye."

Opening the Presentation

What makes some salespeople stand out? The best sales professionals know how to emphasize *benefits* in their presentations. They know that the most effective presentations must start and finish with the prospect's needs and wants as the focus.

Knowledge Development for Planning Presentation Openers

You must practice openers, which are brief introductions to your sales presentation. You must be sure that your openers fit the situation of the particular prospect with whom you are conversing. Practicing openers, like rehearsing any type of presentation, helps to reduce the risks of trial-and-error experience. As you endeavor to build relationships with customers, openers can be critical. You should give attention to the following as you prepare your openers:

- Remind yourself of the lifetime value of the prospect. In other words, think about how much repeat business this customer will give you over the course of a long business relationship.
- Make sure that the right information about the problem-solving offer is ready for presentation. You should include in your preparation appropriate information about your sales organization, the competition, and the business environment.

- Continuously seek out secondary sources of information. Make sure that information about the prospect is up-to-date and that she is aware of issues that might be affecting her position in the market-place.
- Continuously practice questioning and listening techniques to ensure that you ask the right questions and that the information obtained in the answers to those questions is useful.
- Emphasize the importance of ethical behavior with prospects.
- Emphasize the importance of not making promises that cannot be fulfilled.
- Recognize that whatever openers are used, there will likely have to be follow-ups, and the prospect will want to make sure that what was said in the opener comes to pass.

Introductions

All sales presentations need effective, brief introductions, but this is particularly true when you make your first call on a prospect. In your opener, you must introduce yourself, your company, and your reason for calling on the prospect. You can use the following language in designing openers:

- Good morning (afternoon).
- My name is . . .
- I represent . . .
- I am here to . . .

In the opener, show the prospect that you are aware of the prospect's situation and that you have a product that can help his business.

An effective opening statement is essential to getting the prospect's attention. You will find that sometimes a minute or two of friendly conversation relaxes prospects and makes for an effective opening strategy. This opening is most effective when the topic of conversation is planned. The next section will examine some opening techniques that you can use, but first you need to be aware of what the opener must do. Your opener must:

- Convey sincerity and demonstrate your interest in the prospect's situation.

- Stimulate the prospect's desire to listen to the rest of the presentation.
- Clear the prospect's mind of what was on it when you appeared at the door.
- Plant the idea that you are a professional and want to sell—that is, give a preview of the benefits that the prospect can achieve with your help.
- Promote confidence and justify the time you will need to conduct the presentation.
- Plant the seed of an idea or a recommendation that you will develop later in the presentation.
- Pick up facts only the person you are talking to can provide.
- Subtly suggest that you can serve the prospect better than the present supplier.
- Change some of the ways the prospect has been thinking about you or your company.

You must be smart in your choice of words. You must keep your conversation focused. One way to do this is to avoid long, rambling sentences. Further, you should avoid buzzwords, jargon, and qualifiers like "I guess" or "probably," as such words or phrases suggest that you are operating from a weak position.

Show sincere interest in the product *and* the prospect; establish equal power by using the prospect's name fairly frequently; shut up and use active listening skills to learn as much as possible about the prospect and her needs; make developing a relationship more important than making the sale; understand the prospect by uncovering her values. Ask, "What's important to you about . . . ?" types of questions, and be sure to confirm your understanding of what the prospect says.[2]

Attention-Getters

The procedure outlined here for gaining attention takes into consideration the thought process of the prospect and provides an easy flow of thought transference from your mind to the mind of the prospect. You must first clear the prospect's mind of present thoughts and ideas, and then gently guide the prospect into your thought pattern, thus directing the entire meeting.

"If you don't have the prospect's attention, you don't have anything!" This thought is worth remembering.

Here are some basic attention-getters you can use in your openings:

- *Ask something.* "Mr. Countryman, how satisfied are you with your present supplier? My reason for calling is to show you that with my company, you can lower your distribution costs by as much as 25 percent. I would like to discuss this in more detail. Is that okay?"
- *Say something.* "Small business spends 10 percent of its revenue on promotional expenses. I would like to show you how easy it is to target potential customers more effectively, reducing advertising expenditures."
- *Show something.* "This is our newest smartphone. It has the most innovative mobile business applications. This enables your salespeople to gain a competitive edge in the marketplace by optimizing critical business workflow remotely."
- *Give something.* "Good evening. Mrs. Hirschheim of ABC Grocery Company is a friend and also a client of mine, and she feels that this financial guide we offer has been valuable in analyzing her financial situation. We were discussing the possibility of sharing this service with other people in this area, and she suggested that I contact you. It takes only a few minutes to determine whether or not you could benefit from this service. May I continue?"

There are many other kinds of attention-getters; following are some that you will find useful.

The Referral Opener

Obtaining testimonials and referrals is critical to sales success. In addition to getting a prospect's attention, referrals constitute an active, ongoing prospecting function that requires much less cold calling on the part of the sales force. Referrals from existing customers who are known to prospects can open doors to previously off-limits prospects. In the process of getting the prospect's attention, testimonials can change the atmosphere of a presentation from one of skepticism to one of interest.

The referral opener is effective because it makes the prospect feel important. The prospect is flattered and appreciative in knowing that someone has taken the time and effort to obtain information about the prospect's situation, needs, and wants. This immediately sets the approach on a friendly footing. The more exact the information, the more the prospect is impressed; therefore, the more thorough you are in accumulating information, the more likely you are to plan an opener that will strike a responsive chord. The next best thing to selling to a friend is selling to a friend of a friend. The people from whom you get referrals generally fall into the following categories in relation to the prospect.

Casual Acquaintance of Prospect

This source of referral may be a person who has heard of a prospect who lives in the prospect's neighborhood or works in the prospect's building. This person probably does not know enough about the prospect to give specific facts about the situation, but she knows some general information that will help you plan the opener to the approach. This is much better than cold calling. An example of an opener for this type of referral would be:

> Good morning. Are you Mrs. Hunter? Mrs. Hunter, a colleague of yours, Tracia Farmer, was telling me about your plans to expand your business. I thought I'd stop by to show you how my product can help your growth plans.

Personal Friend of Prospect

This type of referral is more effective than a referral to an acquaintance. When a person gives you a referral to a personal friend, that person will usually divulge some joke or incident of a personal nature—something that is not known to everyone. As you relate some of this information to the prospect in the approach, the prospect will accept you in a friendly fashion, and the sales call will be off to a flying start.

Warning: You should not try to get too friendly too quickly. You should let the relationship proceed at the pace the prospect desires.

This type of referral is also effective because the prospect knows that if he refuses the appointment, he runs the risk of offending the friend who gave the referral, and he does not want this to happen. Many times you actually get the appointment because the prospect likes and respects the person who gave you the referral, and not because of any special effort on your part. An example of an opener for this type of referral would be:

Good evening. Are you Mr. Maurin? Mr. Maurin I've had the pleasure of performing a programming service for Michael Martin, your golf buddy, who asked me to tell you about my service. He specifically told me to tell you that it won't improve your golf game, but it might provide the money for a few extra golf lessons. I know you and Mike have had some good times on the golf course.

Use a Known Name

You can use the name of a prestigious personality that the prospect will recognize. Every town and community contains people who are well known and respected. These people are not necessarily the richest, most influential people in the community, but they have earned respect through their positions, usefulness, or value to the people of the area.

Whether they are small business owners, pastors, school teachers, or other outstanding citizens, they have made truly valuable contributions to their communities, churches, civic clubs, or businesses. A referral from this type of person is valuable because it impresses prospects as to your prestige and worth. Prospects usually assume that if a person of such caliber gave you a referral, you must be worth listening to. They are also flattered that a prestigious person has remembered them and referred you to them. You should always strive to get this type of referral. An example of an opener with this type of referral would be:

> Ms. Reese, Mr. McDonald of Liberty Bank is a friend and also a client of mine. He feels that this special service we offer has been valuable in keeping his employees satisfied. We were discussing the possibility of sharing this service with some of the substantial entrepreneurs in this area, and he suggested that I contact you.

Referral Card of Introduction

This attention-getter is very effective when used correctly. Be very careful, however, about the continuity of the thought pattern. Each sentence is important and serves a specific purpose. You should rehearse this technique until it is letter-perfect. You will get a very high ratio of appointments with this technique if it is performed naturally and smoothly. An example of an opener for this attention-getter would be:

Good evening. Are you Mr. Hamilton? Mr. Hamilton, Rolfe McCollister is a friend of yours. Is that right? Rolfe recently asked me to perform a professional service for him that he appreciated very much, and he suggested that I contact you personally and discuss this service with you. He also assured me the courtesy of an appointment and asked me to give you this card.

At this point, you hand the prospect the card of introduction and remain silent until the prospect reads it. Then you say, "Is it possible for us to discuss this now, or would Thursday morning be more convenient?" If you make a later appointment, you should be specific about the time and place.

How do you get referral cards of introduction? You ask for them! When you make a sale or visit a client, you can ask for a referral. If the client gives a referral, then hand the client your business card with a message on the back, so the client can sign it (or have the client write the message). An example of a client's message to a prospect on the back of a business card would be:

JoAnn Burbridge (sales representative) has performed a valuable service for me. She knows what she is talking about, and it would be worth your while to listen to her.

Prospect Benefits

Selling benefits is what the sales presentation is all about. You can use a benefit statement as an effective opener—for example, "Ms. Broome, let me show you how to earn $20,000 more a year by increasing productivity."

In order to use a benefit opener effectively, you must learn as much about the prospect as possible and know that this prospect can benefit from the product or service in the way you describe. Saving money, increasing sales, enhancing security, and improving performance are all benefits that most prospects would agree are desirable. The benefit statement must be brief and general (the details are saved for the heart of the presentation), and preferably demonstrates your advantage over competitors. Here are some examples:

- My name is Judah Dean. I am with ABC Company. We design easy-to-use, affordable tools that are proven to increase profitability for small businesses. We are the only company that offers free in-house training to our customers.

- My name is Ean Hunter and I represent ABC Advertising. We specialize in low-cost, highly effective advertising and promotions for small to medium-sized businesses. We have long been known as a company who treats our customers' advertising dollars as if they are our own.
- My name is Elijah Christopher. My firm, ABC Company, has been in the business of tool sales and rental for over 25 years. We offer our customers the convenience of 24/7 service along with free pick-up and delivery 24/7.

Probing Questions

Sometimes you know what information you need from a prospect but are unable to obtain it. In such circumstances, you can use a probing question as an effective opener—for example, "What would one year of free shipping on bulk orders mean to you, Mr. Jase?" Probing questions should emphasize important buying motives, such as saving money, reducing effort, increasing efficiency, and so on. You can then use the prospect's response to guide the rest of the presentation and to determine additional questions you might wish to ask.

You should ask questions conversationally, and should not treat prospects as if they are on the witness stand. Rapid firing of questions is not effective. Such treatment prompts fear, anger, and mistrust in the prospect—none of which is conducive to a sale. The kind of question asked is also important.

More Attention Getters

This section covers a few more attention-getters that salespeople have used successfully. The list presented here is not exhaustive, but rather illustrates various ways you can gain attention, and should serve to prime the pump so that you can get your own creative ideas flowing. A good preparation exercise is to study all the attention-getters that follow with a single prospect in mind, real or hypothetical.

- *Share an idea.* "Does your present supplier offer a 60-day, money-back guarantee?" Here you will want to ask a question to which you anticipate the answer and know you have a distinct competitive advantage.

- *Share a new success story.* "Enclosed is a copy of a thank-you note from a fellow retail grocery owner who says our last promotion helped him increase revenue by 10 percent."
- *Use a curiosity arouser.* "Ms. Justice, on average, what percentage of satisfied customers stop buying within two years? Our research shows . . ."
- *Make a startling statement.* Startling statements should be designed to shock or startle the prospect, or to reveal a new or unique possibility or situation that personally concerns the prospect or her family, business, or need for buying. For example: "Ms. Gentry, every year businesspeople in your industry lose $3 million to employee turnover, and this figure is growing. This means that something must be done to keep valuable employees."
- *Offer a challenge.* "How much money does it cost you per year in equipment breakdowns? How does this cost affect your overall profit? I challenge you to find a better program than mine—my program saves you money and increases profit."

The Exhibit Opener

The exhibit opener is very effective because it immediately captures the prospect's attention. Many salespeople find it easier to start their approach if the prospect's attention is focused on an exhibit rather than on them. The exhibit can be any tangible object—a calendar, newspaper clipping, magazine article, brochure, or gift. You should always have the exhibit in your hand when you greet the prospect. As you begin to talk, you should move it almost to eye level and continue to move it until the prospect focuses his attention on it. Some examples of exhibit openers are as follows:

Dr. Slaughter, have you had a chance to read this article on Medicare that can affect the retirement benefits of your employees?

Ms. Luedtke, this is the advertisement that will be in Sunday's newspaper. The 50 percent off coupon will be used by 10 percent of the customers shopping in your store. I suggest stocking up on . . .

Ms. Deville, did you have an opportunity to read this letter I sent you last week?

If you refer to something that has been mailed to the prospect, you should have a copy of the mailing piece in your hand. If the prospect hesitates in answering a question about it and becomes embarrassed, you can quickly say, "Well, sometimes these things get misplaced, but I wanted to meet with you and explain it to you personally, so I can answer any questions that you may have."

The Compliment Opener

The compliment opener is effective because it appeals to a basic human instinct. People are starving for a little appreciation and recognition and will do almost anything to get it. In fact, this desire subconsciously influences or controls most of our behavior. Therefore, when you give appreciation in the form of compliments, they fulfill prospects' inner hunger or need for ego satisfaction. A prospect may react with only a smile, shrug, mild remark, or even embarrassment, but nevertheless he will love the compliment. It will make him feel wonderful and immediately want to do something nice for the person who caused this feeling. He will feel obligated to be courteous in return and will reason that the least he can do is listen to you, or perhaps even invite you in.

Again, be forewarned that a thin line exists between a compliment and flattery; the differentiator is sincerity. A flatterer coldly and calculatingly manipulates prospects' emotions for selfish reasons. A prospect can spot this immediately and will seldom grant an appointment to such a person. A sincere compliment is always true, specific, and in good taste. Generally everyone has some good points; your task is to find them. The most effective method of paying a compliment is to quote what someone else has said. You can praise prospects without limits if you are truly repeating what you have heard others say, since such statements will contain no hint of flattery. For example:

Mrs. Turner, I just left a good friend of yours, Elvira Foote, and she's one of your biggest boosters. She said that you are one of the most competent young businesswomen and community leaders in our whole area. She doesn't see how you find time to be a heart fund chairperson, Sunday school teacher, Girl Scout leader, and the operator of a thriving business—but you look like it all agrees with you.

Once you have secured an appointment, made a positive impression, and have effectively opened communication with the prospect, the next step is to begin the groundwork for developing a long-term relationship. By asking the right questions and truly listening to the answers, you will determine the best way to meet the needs of your prospects/customers. This is the focus of the next chapter.

5 *Examination*

Seek first to understand, then to be understood.
—Stephen R. Covey, *The Seven Habits of Highly Effective People*

The Examination Step

Professional selling is more about the asking than the telling. Investigative reporter and author John Sawatsky describes the art of asking questions as follows. The best questions are like clean windows, he asserts: "A clean window gives a perfect view. When we ask a question, we want to get a window into the source. When you put values in your questions, it's like putting dirt on the window. It obscures the view of the lake beyond. People shouldn't notice the question in an interview, just like they shouldn't notice the window. They should be looking at the lake."[1]

Thoughtful questions can make the difference early in the presentation, because they demonstrate your sincere desire to truly understand the issues and goals that the prospect or customer is working to solve or attain. To become a trusted business advisor, you must ask thoughtful questions, probe for a deeper understanding of the concerns behind the prospect's answers, and listen at a very high level before you begin prescribing a potential solution. Remember the old adage: people don't care about what you know until they know that you care.

The work of Charles Green, founder of Trusted Advisor Associates, LLC, has centered on a model of trustworthiness based on the following four components[2]:

- *Credibility.* The words we say, the skills and credentials we bring, and the way in which people experience us make people trust us.
- *Intimacy.* The extent to which people feel they can confide in us, and perceive us as discreet and empathetic make people trust us.

- *Reliability.* The actions we take, our predictability, and the ways in which people find us reliable make people trust us.
- *Self-orientation.* The more people feel we are focused on ourselves, rather than them, the less they trust us.

The basic goals of the examination step are: (1) to build credibility by confirming your understanding of the prospect's situation (based on preparation for the sales call) and to uncover the prospect's latent need(s); (2) to gain the trust of the prospect such that he feels comfortable confiding in you; and (3) to demonstrate that you are a reliable source and a solution provider. You must use examination skills to further your knowledge of prospect/customer needs and wants so you can customize the features of your products/services. By asking the right questions and truly listening to the answers, you can establish the foundation for long-term customer relationships.

The question-asking examination step must be psychologically structured to help uncover: (1) the prospect's primary concern, which is *what* the prospect wants; and (2) the prospect's dominant buying urge, which is *why* the prospect wants it. A prospect's primary concern is the immediate goal representing what the prospect wants. The prospect's dominant buying urge reflects the real reason why the prospect wants or needs what you are offering.

For example, Deborah Ryan, salesperson, understands that Bernard Walker's primary concern is to increase Walker & Associates' sales volume and market share. But why does Mr. Walker want more sales and market share? On a personal level, perhaps he wants to build a new house, educate his children, buy his wife a new car, or plan for long-term financial security. These are all examples of the love-of-family motive, which is a basic dominant buying urge. Someone else may have a high psychological need for achievement and want more sales to achieve recognition and enjoy the prestige of success. On a professional level, it could be that Mr. Walker wants to position his company as a dominant competitor in order to sell the company down the line. The real reason (i.e., the dominant buying urge) is the thing that is psychologically significant to the prospect. Selling is a problem-solving business, a want-satisfying business.

However, even after asking the right questions to determine the prospect's needs and wants, your work will be for nothing if you do not listen effectively to the answers. If someone speaks and no one listens, there has been no communication. Sometimes egos get in the way. That is, while one person is speaking, another may already be mentally formulating what he is going to say when that person finishes speaking. Instead of digesting information, people often are busy thinking only of how best to impress the person who is speaking with their next statement. The result is EgoSpeak: the art of boosting one's own ego by speaking only about what one wants to talk about, and not being sensitive to what another person wants to say. In building trust, however, it's not about you; it's all about the prospect/customer.

This chapter will address both parts of the examination step: the art of questioning prospects to determine their primary concerns and dominant buying urges, and the process of listening effectively to what they say.

The Dominant Buying Urge

Dale Carnegie once said, "There is only one way to get anybody to do anything, and that is by making him [or her] *want* to do it."[3] How can you make prospects want to buy from you? First, you must examine a prospect's psychological want or need, and then you must determine the buying urge that will motivate that prospect to action.

Think about the phrase *dominant buying urge*. Exactly what does it mean? What does each word mean?

- *Dominant:* ruling or controlling
- *Buying:* acquiring or purchasing
- *Urge:* motive or impulse

Thus, the *dominant buying urge* by definition is the "ruling acquiring motive" or "controlling purchasing impulse." It is that inner urge or drive that motivates a prospect to take the action required to consummate a sale. When questioning prospects, your primary goal is to uncover the dominant buying urge within them.

A Structure for Examining

Before you can present a solution, you must thoroughly understand the prospect's problem. Thus, how well you question determines your success in sales. The more creative the questions, the more thought you provoke and the more valuable the information received in reply will be. You must make it easy for prospects to satisfy their primary concern and dominant buying urge.

For example, one common selling approach is for you to ask buyers needs-assessment questions early in the presentation. Such questioning is designed to uncover prospect needs and wants previously unknown to you. You must be careful not to have so much structure in your questioning that you sound mechanical, but enough structure to ensure that your questions obtain needed prospect information. Many new salespeople begin a sales presentation with a questioning approach, only to realize that the entire time allotted for the presentation has been consumed by the question-and-answer process. You must remember to use the information gathered during the needs-discovery step to match the benefits offered by your product or service.

Two general types of questions are used in sales: *open-ended* and *closed-ended*. Open-ended questions begin with *who, what, when, where, how,* and *why*. They cannot be answered with a yes or no. Closed-ended questions *can* be answered with a yes or no. Your mission is to ask as many open-ended questions as possible. Why? Because you want the prospect to talk. To get the prospect to open up, you need to ask open-ended questions.

Questioning Techniques

This section consists of several questioning techniques used to uncover the prospect's dominant buying urge. In using any of these methods, your goal is to listen more and speak less. A general rule of thumb is 80:20; that is, the prospect speaks 80 percent of the time, and you speak 20 percent. This is not easy. You must practice this skill.

Diagnostic and Surgical Inquiries

Like a doctor diagnosing an illness, you can help detect and solve customers' problems by using the different types of inquiries shown in Figure 5.1. These inquiries are broken down into two main types: *diagnostic* and *surgical*.

Diagnostic inquiries are broad and are used to get the prospect/cus-

FIGURE 5.1 Diagnostic and Surgical Inquiries

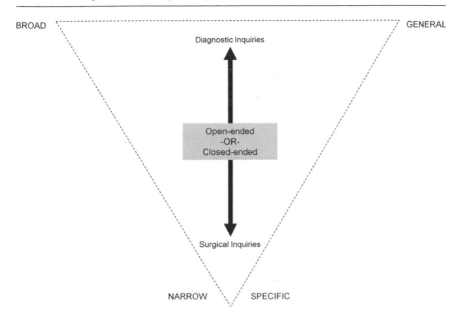

tomer thinking about the general state of affairs regarding her business needs. They are meant to obtain general background for the surgical inquiries that follow. Diagnostic inquiries are also open and begin with "Tell me about . . ." or "Share with me . . ." Here are some examples of diagnostic inquiries:

- "Tell me about the challenges you face promoting the products and services that your organization sells."
- "Share with me the steps that are currently in place for order processing."

When speaking to a top officer of a firm, you can use diagnostic inquiries to elicit that person's vision for the firm and determine how your product or service could help the top officer attain that vision. For example, "What is your vision for making your customers more satisfied?" Once you have obtained the information needed to appeal to the prospect/customer's general needs and desires, the next step is to use surgical inquiries to hone in on more specific issues and/or challenges that pertain to the information you have uncovered with your diagnostic inquiries.

Surgical inquiries are narrow and are used to focus the prospect/customer on specific issues and/or concerns stemming from the general information provided by the prospect/customer. Think of these as follow-up questions. Here are some examples of surgical inquiries:

- "You mentioned earlier that one of the challenges you're facing is promoting your company's products in more efficient ways. Please tell me what you mean, specifically, by *efficient*."
- "You said you don't really have specific steps in place for order processing. Could you tell me how your call center employees communicate with your order fulfillment department when processing customer orders?"

The following is an example of a dialogue between a customer and a salesperson using diagnostic and surgical inquiries:

Salesperson: Please share with me what you are currently doing to address employee turnover in your company. [diagnostic]

Customer: Well, we do what most other companies do, I guess. We try hard to make our employees happy so they won't leave.

Salesperson: Could you tell me specifically what you do to enhance employee satisfaction? [diagnostic]

Customer: My management team and I meet twice a year to discuss every employee and determine what's needed to develop each person and make him more productive. Then we meet with each employee to discuss an action plan that addresses their individual development needs. We hate to lose employees to the competition.

Salesperson: So, preventing the loss of valuable employees to your competition is very important to you? [surgical]

Customer: Of course.

Salesperson: Tell me, in your opinion, what has kept you from retaining every employee? [diagnostic]

Customer: Frankly, some employee turnover is out of our control. Some employees leave because their spouses' careers move them away.

Salesperson: And the others?

Customer: Well, the others leave for what they think are better opportunities.

Salesperson: So, having a cost-effective way of implementing a career awareness and employee retention program, which would help prevent your employees from defecting to the competition, is important to you? [surgical]

Customer: Well, yes.

Salesperson: What value would you place on lowering employee turnover by, say, 10 percent per year? [surgical]

Customer: Ten percent would mean keeping another one hundred employees for whom we've spent $30,000 per person in training. I guess 10 percent would save my company $3 million per year at a minimum.

Salesperson: Ms. Roseburgh, how would you feel about a solution that would cost less than $100,000 per year and would save you that $3 million annual turnover cost?

Remember, the goal is to get to the heart of the prospect's problem without making the prospect feel like he is on the witness stand in court.

Inquiring Questions (IQs)

Inquiring questions are depth-probing questions that can be open-ended or closed-ended. The idea is to dig deeper into the prospect's situation. The following is an example of this type of questioning sequence.

Salesperson: Ms. Rylee, has anyone explained to you all the benefits of using data security software?

Ms. Rylee: Yes.

Salesperson: Well, let's briefly review them.

If Ms. Rylee's answer were no, you would say, "Here's specifically what it will do for you."

Next, try to determine the prospect's area of primary concern (what she wants):

Salesperson: Ms. Rylee, here are the major benefits . . . [these should be neatly listed in a presentation]. Which of these benefits or features suits your situation best? Which do you think is the most important? [digging deeper]

At this point, you should listen—and listen very carefully, because the prospect's answer to this question will reveal her primary concern. You must hear, digest, and evaluate the prospect's answers as she progresses from the primary concern (what she wants) to the dominant buying urge (why she wants it).

Assume Ms. Rylee chooses "peace of mind" as the benefit that is most important to her. You then try to progress from her primary concern (what she wants) to her dominant buying urge (why she wants it). Make this progression by asking:

Salesperson: I am sure you have a good reason for selecting that particular reason. Would you mind telling me *why* you chose it? [digging deeper still]

Ms. Rylee: Our company decided that it is too risky not to have some type of firewall protection on our computer systems. Our data files contain highly sensitive and classified information.

At this point, you would take the final step by responding, "Well, that's why I'm here. A lot of people are concerned about data security today. I'd like to help you gain some peace of mind, just like I've helped others. You have too many other things to concern yourself with than to worry about someone stealing your sensitive and classified company information." [moving into the prescription phase]

The Satisfied Customer Survey

The satisfied customer survey is a survey or an examination that is conducted to poll or question satisfied customers (not prospects) to determine why they do business with you. The survey is another questioning technique that can help you obtain information on why customers buy from you. Gathering and analyzing this information can help you understand prospects' primary concerns (what they want) and dominant buying urges (why they want it). You do this by reviewing the survey and asking prospects to choose which items they think are most important.

To conduct a satisfied customer survey, you first select a representative list of customers. The idea is to try to get information from a cross-section of different types of buyers and users of different types of services. Next, approach an individual customer and tell her that you appreciate her business and value her opinions. Explain that you are constantly trying to improve your customer service, and so you are surveying some of your major accounts. Then you ask, with a smile, "Would you mind sharing with me why you chose our firm to handle your needs?" You should listen carefully to the answer. If the customer makes remarks about you and the sales organization, you should write them down as she talks. Remember, if the customer says it, she then believes it and will defend it. The customer may also share with you some things that have been bothering her, which will give you a chance to answer questions and clear the air. Such an exchange has been known to save accounts because the customer can express concerns that have never before been discussed.

Once you've talked to several customers and have a representative sample of the reasons satisfied customers do business with you, list those reasons, arranging them in the order of importance as reported by the customers. In addition to helping you stay in close contact with customers while monitoring your feelings toward you and the sales organization, such a list gives you a potent question-asking tool to be used with prospects.

Here is an example of how this works. Share the information with a prospect by showing her the list and asking questions as follows:

> *Salesperson:* Ms. Clack, a satisfied customer survey was recently completed to determine why our customers choose to do business with us. Here's what they told us. [Review the list with prospect.] Which one of these do you think is the most important to *your company*? Which one would you choose? If you have something completely different in mind, we can put it in the space at the bottom of this list.

The prospect will select one or sometimes two or more items from the list. This should help you determine the prospect's immediate or primary concern—that is, what the prospect wants. When the prospect selects an item, you should ask the prospect why she chose that particular one. Here you hope to get some insight into the prospect's dominant buying urge— that is, why the prospect wants what she wants. For example:

> *Salesperson:* Ms. Clack, it is interesting that you chose number of markets served. Why did you choose that particular one? [open-ended question]

Once again, you must listen, and listen carefully, to the prospect's answer and try to pick up some clue that might reveal her dominant buying urge. Suppose the prospect answers, "Because we are expanding and penetrating new markets, which will increase our production by 50 percent." The prospect's primary concern in this case is doing a good job that will penetrate new markets and, she hopes, increase company profits, perhaps so her profit-sharing check will be greater. The prospect's dominant urge (the real reason she wants what she wants) is, perhaps, getting more take-home pay, because this will give her a greater sense of financial security. Maybe Ms. Clack plans to use the profit-sharing money to help make a down payment on a new home. You have to keep probing in order to learn both the business and personal reasons for buying.

The "If" Technique

You must determine why your prospects want to buy your product—the real reason, the driving force that will motivate them to action. Here is a series of questions to help you determine exactly what a prospect wants and why the prospect wants it. These examples preface the answer to the prospect's apparent problem with an "if":

- "If you were the CEO of this company, what would be the first thing you would change about . . .?"
- "If it were possible for you to take care of your trucks and your warehouses through our warranty, you'd have more coverage—one policy that provides security and savings!"

In the following examples, varying techniques are used:

- "This savings, as shown in our proposal, would mean better than 5 percent to you. What would this 5 percent savings mean to you and your company?"
- "If you had that money now, you wouldn't have any trouble knowing what to do with it, would you? Would you mind telling me just one of the things you would like to do with it?

To encourage the prospect to answer, you may need to suggest first what he personally would do with the money:

Salesperson: Mr. Edward, if you had the $1,000 now, representing your savings, you wouldn't have any trouble knowing what to do with it, would you? I'd sure like to have one of those new wireless notepads you mentioned earlier. Mr. Edward, what would it be like to lower your operating costs, have the new computer you've wanted, and have peace of mind knowing you have everything covered under our warranty?

After the prospect responds to this, you say, "Well, that's why I'm here, to help you do just that."

Situation, Problem, Implication, and Need-Payoff Questions

Neil Rackham popularized a questioning technique known as SPIN, which stands for *situation, problem, implication, and need-payoff.*[4] This framework is very useful for structuring questions used early in the presentation. The idea is to move from a general question to a very specific question that focuses the prospect on his dominant buying urge, similar to the diagnostic and surgical questioning technique described earlier. Visualize a funnel, which starts with the situation question, moves to the problem question, down to the implication question, and, finally, to a permission-to-proceed question: the need-payoff (see Figure 5.2).

Here is an example of how the SPIN technique is used. After you've exchanged pleasantries with the prospect, proceed as follows:

Salesperson: Mr. Mincks, I noticed in the newspaper that your company is rapidly expanding through mergers and acquisitions. How has this strategy worked so far? [situation question]

You should listen carefully to the prospect's answer, and then continue in this manner:

Salesperson: Interesting. Based on my research, I've noticed that most mergers experience problems with combining company cultures. How has your company handled this issue? [problem question]

Let the prospect talk while listening for clues to problems, issues, concerns, and challenges. Then continue with:

Salesperson: It sounds like you have a good plan to integrate the employees of the other company with your workforce. However, one of the concerns you

FIGURE 5.2 The SPIN Questioning Strategy

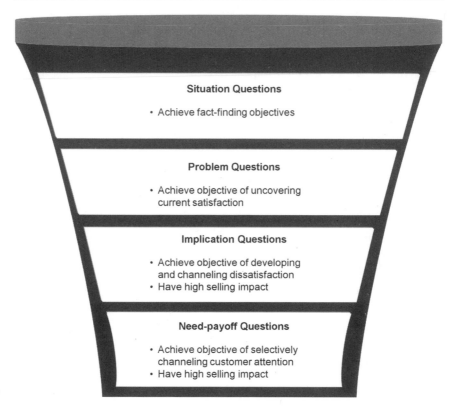

Source: Adapted from Rackham, Neil (1989), *Major Account Sales Strategy*. New York: McGraw Hill

mentioned is the possibility of losing some of the employees because of the change. What percentage of the total workforce do you think you might lose? [problem question]

After getting the answer, you then show concern for the prospect's challenges:

Salesperson: Ten percent of a thousand employees can be devastating for most companies. How would losing one hundred employees affect your ability to provide exceptional service to your customers? [implication question]

Again, you must show genuine concern. Empathize by thinking about what would happen to you if you were in your prospect's shoes. What would be going through your mind if you had this problem? What would be your concerns? How would you handle this problem? Notice how the implication question links the problem to a larger concern—in this case, serving the prospect's customers. Implication questions should be linked to such broader issues as profitability, market share, customer satisfaction, peace of mind, and so on. Once you have uncovered the dominant buying urge, you should summarize the prospect's concerns and ask for permission to present a solution by saying something like the following:

> *Salesperson:* In summary, Mr. Mincks, you said that your merger and acquisition strategy appears to be working fine. However, you're concerned about losing some valuable employees during the merger process. Your estimate is one hundred employees lost due to the change. You are concerned about the impact of this loss on your company's ability to serve its customers. If I can show you a cost-effective way of hiring employees who are already experienced in your industry, which could provide you with a backup plan, would you be interested? [need-payoff question]

This question should be the *only* closed-ended question you use in the SPIN sequence. Once you have received permission to continue, you can move to the presentation.

A note of caution is necessary here. Salespeople have overused the need-payoff question that is structured: "If I can show you . . . would you be interested?" Therefore, you should vary it somewhat. For example, you might say, "Mr. Mincks, in summary, you are concerned about . . . With your permission, I'd like to present a possible solution. Is that okay?" The point is that you guide the prospect through SPIN by asking well thought-out questions, showing that you have done some research on the prospect's situation (implying that the prospect's problem is larger than first thought), and asking for permission to present your solution. That is the essence of SPIN.

Regardless of the questioning technique used, you must make sure that your presentations fit your prospects' wants or needs. Ask well thought-out questions at the right time. Asking questions keeps prospects involved in the presentation. Rather than saying, "So, that's why you bought the XYZ system," you can change the statement into a question: "What were your other considerations, if any, when you purchased the XYZ system?" Remember, questions are the main tool in your tool kit.

Reacting during the Questioning Stage

When asking questions and probing for needs, salespeople who are empathetic are better able to understand their prospects' motives. This is done in a combination of ways, including the following:

1. Receiving verbal and nonverbal signals that reveal true needs.
2. Processing these signals to gain insight into the prospect's situation.
3. Using the information received from signals to develop probing questions to gain further insight into the prospect's situation.
4. Convincing prospects that their needs are being communicated and understood.
5. Uncovering latent needs.
6. Responding with problem-solving solutions.

When prospects ask *you* tough questions at this stage, you should do the following:

1. *Restate the question.* Even if you understand it, you should say, "So what you're asking is . . ." The prospect may clarify her concern or answer her own question the second time around.
2. *Ask "What do you think?" or "What makes you ask?"* That throws attention back to the prospect, giving you precious seconds to compose your response.
3. *Start with a general reply.* For example, you may say, "The quick answer is . . . ," and then gauge to what extent the prospect wants to hear more detail. Some people will accept the preliminary answer and move on.
4. *Do not fake it.* If you need more time or information to answer the question effectively, you should say so. You can tell the prospect that you would like some time to research the issue and ask if it would be okay to reply to the question within twenty-four hours. Most people would rather wait for a good answer later than listen to a bad one on the spot.

In a sales presentation, you should strive to convince a prospect that your offering is the best available solution for the needs expressed by the prospect. During the presentation, you must "check the pulse" of prospects regularly. You must remain alert for any signals that prospects may send. You cannot be so rehearsed that buying signals are ignored. It is your responsibility to listen to buyers during the presentation so that buyer motivations can be uncovered. Question-based presentations are the link between your ability to listen and your ability to uncover buyer motivations.

Listening

"No, we haven't had any in a long time now," said the supermarket clerk.

"Whoa!" said a store manager who was just walking by. "I'm sure we have, lady. This is a new clerk. He doesn't know how we keep our inventory and stock records. We've got plenty in the warehouse, and we'll get some over this afternoon. If you come back after lunch, we'll have all you need. Now, tell me, what was it that he said we haven't had in a long time?"

"Rain," said the woman.

No matter what you do, a good deal of your day is spent listening. By listening to your prospect, you show respect for the prospect's position. Consider the following, and then ask yourself if the average person's listening skills are good or bad:

- People use ¼ of their listening capacity.
- People use ¹⁄₁₀ of their memory potential.
- People forget ½ of what they have heard within eight hours.
- Eventually, people forget 95 percent of what they have heard unless cued by something later on.
- People usually distort what little they do remember.

This is not a resounding commentary on our ability to listen. Put in a selling context, if you spend six hours a day with prospects, you might spend three hours hearing them. In that case, you would:

- Actually listen to only 90 minutes of conversation.
- Remember only 45 minutes of conversation within 8 hours.
- Remember only 18 minutes of the day's conversation after 8 hours.

You can never learn anything while talking. You need to *listen* to pick up buying clues.

Listening is a trainable skill requiring three things: (1) a sense of how well one listens; (2) some motivation to improve; and (3) practice. Poor listening conveys a lack of interest, boredom, and perhaps even hostility. Alternatively, good listening has the power to draw people in and make them feel valued and understood.

Good listening is an art. Following are some ways to help you practice good listening[5] and demonstrate it when in front of prospects:

- You can push something aside (put down a briefcase or pull an order form off the desk) to signal that the prospect has your full attention.
- You should nod or tilt your head when prospects make important points.
- You should take notes, as that sends the message that what is important to the prospect is important to you.
- You must show interest without interrupting too much. You can show interest by saying things like "Incredible," "Now I understand," or "That's really something."

Table 5.1 lists twelve types of poor listeners. You should ask yourself which one best describes your own listening style.

Listening versus Hearing

How many people get lost because they only half-listen to a set of travel directions? Listening is not the same as hearing. Although a person must hear in order to listen, a person who is hearing is not necessarily *listening*. Hearing is a function carried out by the brain, wherein the sounds received by the ears are assigned meaning. But just because the brain understands words does not mean that the mind understands what is received.[6]

People's minds are much faster than their mouths. The average person in the United States speaks between 150 and 200 words a minute, depending on the geographic region. Average listeners think four times faster than that. So, the mind can process information much faster than the mouth can speak.[7] This speaking-listening differential not only can result in a lack of interest, but it also can cause people to prejudge what they are hearing. If a speaker is uninteresting, dull, or abrasive, these perceptions will cause the listener to judge the speaker and mentally elaborate on what the speaker

TABLE 5.1 Why We Do Not Hear What Others Say

If you want to listen so you really hear what others say, make sure you are not a:

Mind Reader:	You hear little or nothing as you think, "What is this person really thinking or feeling?"	**Comparer:**	When you get sidetracked assessing the messenger, you are sure to miss the message.
Rehearser:	Your mental tryouts for "Here's what I'll say next" so you tune out the speaker.	**Derailer:**	Changing the subject too quickly tells others you are not interested in anything they have to say.
Filterer:	Selective listening means you hear only what you want to hear.	**Sparrer:**	You hear what is said but quickly belittle or discount it.
Dreamer:	Drifting off during a face-to-face conversation can lead to an embarrassing "What did you say?" or "Could you repeat that?"	**Placater:**	Agreeing with everything you hear just to be nice or to avoid conflict does not mean you are a good listener.
Identifier:	If you refer everything you hear to your experience, you probably did not really hear what was said.	**Stereotyper:**	Based on preconceived ideas and stereotypes, you selectively listen to words and phrases that confirm your assumptions.
Corrector:	Your focus is on correcting the other person's grammar to such an extent that you miss the content of the message.	**Elaborator:**	Your mind races with vivid mental elaborations of what the other person is saying to the point of missing the main message.

Source: Adapted from M. McKay, M. Davis, and P. Fanning, *Messages: The Communication Skills Book* (Oakland, Calif.: New Harbinger Press, 1983), 16–19.

says through attitudinal filters. If the first few words do not hook the listener, the listener will rapidly tune out and think of something else.

Stages in the Listening Process

Effective listening consists of three discrete dimensions, or stages, in the listening process: sensing, processing, and responding. Sensing refers to the actual receipt of messages, processing refers to activities that occur in the mind of the listener, and responding involves acknowledgment that the message has been received. The classic model of communication is a cycle in which messages are being encoded and decoded continuously. Communication is an ongoing give-and-take of shared information, which requires feedback. If a person purposefully or accidentally gives no feedback, the sender will have no idea, or will have a distorted idea, of how well he is communicating. One type of distorted feedback occurs when the listener (receiver) agrees with the speaker (sender) even though she has no clue what the speaker is trying to say.

Sensing is the most basic aspect of listening and involves hearing words, inflection, speed of speech, tone of voice, and noticing nonverbal signals (e.g., body language and facial expressions). Processing refers to what goes on in the mind of the listener as he assigns meaning to incoming messages (decoding). During processing, the message is transformed and organized into a useable form. At this stage, the listener understands the meaning of the message, interprets the underlying implications, evaluates the importance of the various cues, and remembers the message by updating existing information stored in memory. Your primary task when evaluating a message is to prioritize the information coming from the prospect so that you can concentrate on the prospect's key concerns. Responding refers to the information that you send back to the prospect to indicate that the prospect's message has been received correctly.

You must seek feedback to ensure that what you are hearing and saying is being interpreted correctly. This means that you must listen very closely to what prospects say. You must listen and not make assumptions. You should summarize and clarify what you hear by restating or paraphrasing what prospects say. You also should ask many trial close questions. Following is an example of summarizing and clarifying what you hear:

> Let me make sure I understand what you're saying, Ms. Adams. You mentioned that your current supplier rarely provides updated information about the marketplace. In other words, you would like more information more regularly about how your business is performing compared to your industry. Is it safe to say that you view this as a critical part of the salesperson's job? And because your current supplier does not provide certain information consistently, you're thinking about switching suppliers? Do I understand you correctly? If you could be convinced that your next supplier would provide you with market activity information regularly, how would you feel about switching today?

The key to improved listening is using the "extra" time available in the hearing process. As you listen to prospects, you should examine what is being said, question your understanding of what is being said, and involve yourself in the conversation. You also must learn to decipher nonverbal communication. You should give positive verbal cues such as "Hmmm, interesting," "Tell me more, please," and "What did you do next?" You should also mention the prospect's name frequently, but do not overuse it; this can sometimes sound scripted and become annoying to some prospects. Nonverbally, you can show you are a skilled listener by maintaining steady eye contact. You'll become a superb salesperson when you demonstrate good listening skills.

Three Levels of Listening

Concentrate! Experienced buyers can spot a new salesperson almost immediately by the salesperson's listening skills. You must work on listening closely. The skill is harder to master than one would think. Research has shown that there are three levels of listening: *marginal, evaluative,* and *active* listening. At the most basic level, marginal listening, recipients hear the words but are easily distracted and may allow their minds to wander. A classic case of this occurs when new salespeople begin their sales careers. Often, they are so focused on what they are going to say next that they do not truly tune in to what the prospect is saying. Salespeople who listen on a marginal level may miss a name or a key point because their attention is not focused. Consequently, they may miss golden opportunities to trial close. Most important, however, is that they miss opportunities for building trust with prospects because prospects feel that their concerns are not important to the salesperson.

Evaluative listening is an improvement over marginal listening, because the listener is concentrating on what is being said. However, evaluative listeners do not sense what is being communicated nonverbally or through more subtle verbal cues. They are not perceptive in their processing because they focus on literal meaning. You must stay alert and listen for the messages between the lines. You must tune in to what is said and to what is *not* said.

Active listening is a process in which the listener receives messages, processes them, and responds so as to encourage further communication. Listening at this level allows one to draw out more information because the listener is using all of her senses. Active-empathetic listening takes active listening to a higher level. Active-empathetic listening is a process whereby you (the listener) receive verbal and nonverbal messages, process the messages cognitively, respond to them verbally and nonverbally, and attempt to assess the underlying meaning intuitively by putting yourself in the customer's place throughout the sales presentation. Empathy is the ability to put yourself in someone else's shoes.

Table 5.2 lists good and poor listening habits. You should see whether any of these habits apply to people you know, and evaluate which ones apply to you as well. Listen at a deeper level. You must listen for the emotional content of the message and empathize with prospects. Seek to get to the root of prospects' concerns. Remember that nonverbal communication is processed almost unconsciously. By becoming consciously aware of another's tone of voice, posture, gestures, and facial expressions, you will greatly improve your level of understanding.

Listening Attentiveness

Prospects want to be heard. You should listen to them without interruption. You should always allow them to state their position completely. Consider the following statement: "I never said that I needed this product." This seems like a very simple, straightforward statement. Consider how its meaning changes when the inflection is placed on different words:

- "*I* never said that I needed this product." (someone else may have said so)
- "I never *said* that I needed this product." (but I may have implied a need)
- "I never said that I *needed* this product." (but I may want it)

You should ask yourself: How attentive a listener am I? Consider what your responses would be to each of the following questions:

1. *Are you easily bored or distracted?* If so, your attention span is too short. Many sales presentations last for an hour or more. You must

TABLE 5.2 Habits to Differentiate Good from Poor Listening

Good Listener	Poor Listener
• Takes time to think about what the prospect is saying and listens carefully to his tone of voice and inflections	• Tends to be easily distracted with slow speakers and wants to complete the prospect's sentences
• Finds the relevance of what the prospect is saying to the features and benefits of the product/service he is offering	• Mentally "tunes out" or daydreams while the prospect is speaking
• Listens beyond differences in dialect and concentrates on the content of the message	• Distracted by language differences and differences in dialect, and thereby loses track of the message content
• Jots down bullet points of the important points in the conversation while maintaining good eye contact	• Tries to write down every word of the prospect's points but misses the main points
• Does not present a solution until the picture of the prospect's situation is complete	• Quick to give a presentation without a thorough understanding of the prospect's situation
• Holds eye contact and shows enthusiasm (e.g., verbally and nonverbally)	• Lethargic, uninterested, bored, and boring
• Listens for central ideas	• Misses central ideas because of noncritical information

Source: Adapted from M. McKay, M. Davis, and P. Fanning, *Messages: The Communication Skills Book* (Oakland, Calif.: New Harbinger Press, 1983), 16–19.

be able to focus your attention on the prospect for that entire time. Therefore, you should concentrate on eliminating all distractions.

2. *Do you withhold responses by not looking at the talker or by maintaining a blank look?* Maintaining eye contact with prospects is critical. Listen with your ears *and* your eyes.

3. *Do you get impatient and interrupt others?* It is important to let prospects talk. You should let your prospects tell the whole story.

4. *Do you focus on the other person's appearance or delivery to the exclusion of content and ideas?* You must react to a prospect's ideas, not to the prospect. You must not allow things that irritate you about prospects to distract you.

5. *Do you focus on verbal content to the exclusion of the prospect's non-*

verbal cues? Remember, prospects provide much information by non-verbal communications. You want the whole picture, not just part of it.

6. *Do you listen with one ear while mentally planning a rebuttal?* People who do this are not listening. Prospects do not react favorably to responses that do not answer their questions.

7. *Do you consciously practice listening skills?* If you do not practice listening, you will not develop the skill.

8. *Do you ever ask for feedback on how others rate you as a listener?* If you do not, you should start asking.

9. *Do you limit your own talking?* You cannot talk and listen at the same time.

10. *Do you empathize with your prospects, or think like them?* A salesperson who does this understands and retains information better than one who does not.

11. *Do you ask questions to clarify what you do not understand?*

12. *Do you take notes?* Taking notes will help you remember important points.

In uncovering buyer motivations, empathetic salespeople are more likely than others to recognize potential problems early in the presentation. They are sensitive to the concerns voiced by the prospect and are less likely to ignore possible prospect problems. Empathetic salespeople establish quality relationships with customers because they make sure that prospects believe their motivations are being heard and understood. In completing the questioning, listening, and observing cycle, it is important for you to understand basic nonverbal communication.

Nonverbal Communication

Communication takes place on many levels simultaneously. It includes vocal qualities, such as tone of voice and accents, as well as body language—facial expressions, gestures, and attitudes. Roughly 55 percent of communication is body language, or nonverbal communication.[8] Thirty-eight percent of our feelings and attitudes are communicated via the tone of our voice, and only 7 percent of our feelings and attitudes are communicated with words.[9] In other words, more information is communicated nonverbally than through any other form of communication.

Body Language

Most basic communication gestures are the same all over the world. When people are happy, they smile; when they are sad or angry, they frown or scowl. Although some cultures translate these gestures as having the opposite meaning, nodding the head is almost universally used to indicate "yes" or affirmation. Shaking the head from side to side to indicate "no" is also almost universal.

All people have the ability to understand gestures; however, most people hardly pay attention to them. To have success in sales, you must closely observe gestures. For example, you should watch the prospect's mouth. A smile is obviously a positive signal, and a frown a negative signal. You also should observe whether the person's lips are pressed together or relaxed and comfortable, and whether the person shows signs of happiness or of discontent. You should watch to see whether the prospect is maintaining eye contact with you or losing interest. When people are interested, they maintain eye contact. When people cannot express their honest feelings, they usually cannot hold eye contact. You must make sure that *you* maintain eye contact with prospects.

Reading body language is not an exact science, but it does give you some insight into what the prospect is thinking and feeling. You need to read body language carefully. You should practice observing people and should become increasingly conscious of the subtle signs exhibited by prospects and clients. One of the most serious mistakes a novice in body language can make is to interpret a solitary gesture in isolation from other gestures or other circumstances. Remember, gestures must be examined together in order to draw accurate conclusions from them. Gestures invariably tell the truth about a person's feelings or attitudes. A perceptive salesperson can read a person's nonverbal communication and accurately match it to that person's verbal communication. In sales, it is vitally important to read body language.

Reading and Reacting to Nonverbal Signals

Nonverbal signals are processed at a subconscious level. Paying attention to prospects' body language can help you get inside the heads of your prospects. And the inside of the prospect's head is your workshop.

Gerhard Gschwandtner, the founder and CEO of *Selling Power* magazine, developed a training course through scientific research and analysis of thousands of selling situations in Europe and the United States. The course combines nonverbal communication techniques with professional selling skills. To improve your own verbal and nonverbal selling power, you must learn how to read and react to prospects' nonverbal signals. There are five major nonverbal communication channels:[10]

1. Body angle
2. Face
3. Arms
4. Hands
5. Legs

Gschwandtner divides these communication channels (nonverbal expressions) into three types of nonverbal signals—red, *stop;* yellow, *proceed with caution;* and green, *go ahead*—that aid you in responding to a prospect's hidden feelings or attitudes (see Figure 5.3).

FIGURE 5.3 Nonverbal Signals

CHANNELS	SIGNALS					RESPONSE
	Face	Arms	Hands	Legs	Body angle	
RED You should stop selling, express understanding, redirect your approach and build the relationship.	• Angry • Determined • Flush • Tense • Head Shaking • "No"	• Tightly Crossed • Thrust out	• Fists • Pointed finger "stop sign"	• Tightly crossed away from you • Foot stomping	• Leaning far back and away from you • Thrust toward you	• *Express understanding* • *Redirect approach* • *Smile and relax* • *Ask more questions* • *Prevent red signals*
YELLOW Many buyers are able to control their facial expressions, so you must search for additional clues and scan all nonverbal communication channels.	• Tense • Displeased • Skeptical • Superior • Doubtful • Guarded • Frustrated	• Crossed • Tense	• Clasped • Tense • Fidgeting with objects or body parts	• Crossed away from you	• Leaning away from you	• *Relax* • *Respond with a positive green signal* • *Ask questions* • *Listen with empathy* • *Be aware*
Never begin a sales presentation with a buyer who communicates "yellow." Use open-ended questions to encourage and promote conversation.						
GREEN Your prospect is open to you and your selling strategy.	• Friendly • Smiling • Enthusiastic	• Relaxed • Open	• Relaxed • Open	• Uncrossed or crossed toward you	• Upright or directed toward you	• *Smile* • *Be relaxed & friendly* • *Use open-palm gestures* • *Sit or stand with uncrossed legs* • *Look directly at client; head tilted slightly*

Source: Adapted from information in the following e-book: *Reading Your Customers' Buying Signals,* by Gerhard Gschwandtner, from the editors of *Selling Power,* http://www.sellingpower.com, 2002

Is the Prospect Listening?

You need to know whether the prospect is listening. Poor listeners will exhibit some or all of the following behaviors:

- Looking over the salesperson's shoulder or to the side in search of something more interesting.
- Rarely smiling.
- Crossing their arms.
- Putting their hands on their hips.
- Tapping their fingers.
- Checking the clock on the wall or glancing at their watch.
- Picking imaginary lint off their clothes.
- Giving an occasional "Uh-huh" or "I see."
- Using phrases like "Reminds me of the time" or "We all have problems."
- Challenging insignificant details.
- Scowling or staring with a blank look.

Sales success depends upon how well you can modify your personal behavior to adapt to situations quickly. When you see negative nonverbal communication in a prospect, you must adjust your presentation. You should stop talking and ask the prospect an open-ended question to get her engaged in the presentation again. An example of an open-ended question is: "Ms. Jaiden, how do you feel about what I've told you so far?" Remember, open-ended questions begin with *who, what, when, where, how,* and *why.*

When a prospect is closed off, you should focus on increasing her comfort zone and leading her back into the presentation. One easy way to increase a person's comfort zone when that person is closed off is to utilize mirroring—a technique by which you observe the prospect's behavior and then, in a subtle way, act in the same manner in which the prospect is acting. If the prospect's arms are crossed, you should sit back, relax a little, and cross your own arms.

When you notice positive body language, you should keep on track and move in the direction of closure. If prospects are sending negative signs, you should step back and ask more questions. To create more positive energy, you can continually reiterate ideas and validate understanding. You also can review what you have discussed with prospects and validate it by asking clarifying questions.

One way to learn how to interpret body language is to set aside at least fifteen minutes a day to read and study the gestures of other people. You can go to social events, and just sit quietly and watch. Turning off the sound on the television and watching the nonverbal communication is also a good way to practice interpreting others' communication. By turning the sound back on every five minutes or so, you can check the accuracy of your interpretations.

Though it is important for you to observe prospects' body language, it is critical for you to pay close attention to your own. For example, you should avoid slumping, tapping your feet, and so on. These behaviors can send the wrong signals. Instead, you should sit upright, lean forward slightly, and show concern and enthusiasm.

It is necessary to develop the ability to uncover the root cause of your prospect's problem, not just the symptoms associated with the problem. A doctor can just treat the symptoms, but a *specialist* will thoroughly examine her patient to uncover the root cause and then prescribe a specific solution.

The next chapter builds on the examination phase of the sales process. Your specialized knowledge, based on the information you've gathered so far, enables you to prescribe a solution to your prospect's specific business problems.

6 *Prescription*

It isn't that they can't see the solution. It is that they can't see the problem.
—G. K. Chesterton, *Scandal of Father Brown* (1935)

The Prescription Step

In the prescription stage of a sales presentation, your objective is to incite a prospect's interest by showing that you understand the prospect's problem and then prescribe a solution to it. This particular phase is the actual sales presentation, in which you customize your presentation of product features and benefits to the prospect's specific needs and wants. By expressing concern about the prospect personally and confirming your understanding of the prospect's needs, wants, and problems, you display a knowledgeable role and can begin earning the right to become a trusted advisor to the prospect.

The key word of the prescription stage is *concern*—concern for, and a proper understanding of, the prospect's problem. If the prospect has not already recognized the problem or you cannot make the prospect aware of one, then you simply do not have a prospect. There must be some lack, want, or need that is creating a problem for the prospect. The prescription step is where you make full use of the information you gathered in the preparation and examination steps in order to present an optimal solution to the prospect.

The prescription stage also signals the start of the business partnering between buyer and seller. Business partnering occurs as a result of sellers and buyers pooling resources in a trusting atmosphere that is focused on continuous and mutual gain. True partnerships require an understanding of each other's needs and capabilities so that the partners can establish a mutually acceptable vision for the future. In other words, when a seller and buyer know each other's goals and can cooperate in achieving mutually agreed-upon goals, they both should be more willing to invest in the relationship. Thus, as the customer moves toward goal attainment, the supplier moves toward the same goal. This is the epitome of a great partnership.

The Importance of Communication in Prescribing Solutions

The salesperson is charged with the task of meeting customer expectations and needs. In order to provide an answer to a customer's problem, you must completely understand the problem, which requires effective communication. Each communication must bring knowledge and business insights to the prospect. In general, communications that focus on benefits and value are viewed as quality communications. By communicating well, you can be a critical factor in the buyer's decision process during the prescription stage, as well as at all other stages.

By way of introduction, and as a reminder, your prescription should include the following:

1. *Facts about your product/service.* You must have thorough product knowledge.
2. *Your company history.* Focus on evidence of growth and high-quality product and service offerings.
3. *Knowledge of competitors' strengths and weaknesses.* You must know where your product stands so you can determine if your prospect is accurate in his knowledge of competitors' offerings.
4. *Knowledge of your prospect.* You must be familiar with your prospect's business history, main products, main customers, and *their* customers' needs and wants.

Preparation for Prescription

Preparation is not completed once you have planned a presentation. You can always improve it. When you are prepared, you will appear professional. In order to be agile and effective, preparation and sales strategy require creativity, enthusiasm, and perfection. The prescription stage demands the same qualities. Sometimes the first solutions you develop during preparation turn out to be inadequate. In the prescription stage, you will often discover that there is more than one way to arrive at an acceptable solution. As you prepare, here are a few things to keep in mind:

1. *Avoid groveling.* Saying, "We are truly grateful for the opportunity to visit and tender a proposal" may sound polite, but it puts you in a subordinate position. A simple "Thank you for the opportunity to present" will suffice.

2. *Be prepared to provide accurate time frames for delivery and completion of other key aspects of your sale.* Don't make promises you cannot keep, as unkept promises erode your trusted advisor status.

3. *Provide sufficient details about all aspects of your product as needed.* Make sure the prospect can easily follow these details, but do not ramble on without engaging the prospect in dialogue. Giving too much information at the beginning can be as damaging as too little information.

4. *Describe all benefits that a prospect can expect to realize.* Does the prospect personally benefit? Does she benefit in her role in the company? Does her organization benefit?

5. *Present costs of your products and services.* You will eventually have to be very detailed to prevent any misunderstandings and surprises.

Asking the Right Questions

In preparing a solution, you can develop a list of questions that will help to match your product's benefits to your prospect's needs. Asking a few questions such as these will help you perform well:

1. What can I say to convince my prospect that my product is best for his needs?
2. What can I say to convince my prospect that my company is the best supplier?
3. What can I say to convince my prospect that my price is right?
4. What can I say to convince my prospect that today is the day to buy?
5. What answers can I give the prospect to questions about price, quality, and performance?
6. What specific benefits will my prospect realize from my product?
7. What do I do when the prospect mentions my competition?
8. What do I do when the prospect insists on my competition?

As an agile salesperson, you must learn to anticipate prospects' concerns and prepare answers before meeting with them.

Polishing Your Story

Any presentation can be polished, and the first place to start is with your attitude. You must really believe that your product will help your customers. If you do, you will see your customers as friends to whom you are bringing good news. This may sound clichéd, but it is very helpful.

You will succeed more often if you are honestly convinced that potential buyers will be better off by using your product or service. If you believe this, then your task of convincing the prospect becomes easier. This means speaking in terms of benefits to the buyer.

Another way for you to polish your sales presentations is to make sure you have made it easy for prospects to listen. For example, doctors do not have much time to waste, so pharmaceutical salespeople usually cannot present a long list of features and benefits. Instead, they must stress one or two benefits that might influence the doctor, who does not actually buy the product but will prescribe it to patients if convinced of the drug's benefits (e.g., greater effectiveness or fewer side effects).

To effectively use prospects' time during sales presentations, you should identify the actions you want prospects to take and then prepare your presentations so that these actions follow logically and without strain. Perhaps style or color choices can be made early in the sales conversation. Decisions about delivery and methods of payment are best kept for later in the presentation. If you want the prospect to feel fabric or participate in a software demonstration, you should plan accordingly. If information from the prospect is needed, you should plan to ask for it at the appropriate time and make it easy for the prospect to supply the information—for example, by filling in the appropriate blank on an order form or checking an appropriate response.

No amount of polish will offset poor presentation of your information. Consequently, the first time a prospect listens to your presentation should not be the first time you do it. You should rehearse it more than once. You can record your presentations and listen to them, asking yourself: Do I sound nervous? Theatrical? Verbose? Unsure? Your goal is to be confident, relaxed, poised, and concise. You might also practice in front of a mirror a few times to be sure your facial expressions and gestures are appropriate. Once you think the presentation is in pretty good shape, you might want to try it on your spouse, a friend, or another salesperson—even your sales manager. Try not to be too defensive about criticisms from those who listen to rehearsals of the presentation, but instead work to develop your strengths and shore up your weak spots.

Be familiar with your firm's website, catalogs, demonstrators, and visual aids. You should ask yourself: Do I know where to find a particular model in the catalog? Can I navigate my company's website with ease? Do I know where the switch is to turn on my demonstrator? Do I have the slides in order? Do I have all the forms I will need, and a pen that writes? Do I have a copy of my presentation saved on a USB flash drive or a hard copy of my presentation, just in case of a computer glitch? These may seem like obvious and even trivial questions; however, every experienced salesperson has an embarrassing story to tell about the time he did not fully prepare for a sales presentation. Covering all bases in this manner will help you create a more polished presentation.

You will know you have progressed from the examination stage to the prescription stage when a prospect acknowledges that a problem exists. The prospect may ask, "How much can I expect to save in network costs by consolidating all our communications onto a single infrastructure?" or "Level with me, now. Could your company actually deliver in ten days?" The foreperson may want to hear about maintenance schedules or terms of payment. The retailer may want to hear that the new display rack will increase sales by 20 percent, not that other retailers are very pleased with it. The physician may want to be reassured that the new drug causes no uncomfortable side effects; its higher price might be of no consequence. The purchasing agent may be interested in the quantity discount on a particular shipment of chemicals, rather than in their caustic properties. The key in all buying situations is to convert your capabilities into advantages as you prescribe solutions to your prospects' problems.

You will be helped in your prescription by using some of the following suggestions:

1. *Ask your prospect if anything has changed since you last communicated.* For example, the prospect may have talked with a competitor and then can present some new hurdles for you to overcome. You do not want to be surprised during your presentation.
2. *Ask the prospect to tell you where they are in their decision process.* For example, if you are the first of four competitive presenters, you are

not likely to sell after your presentation. Your prospects want to compare, so use this as an opportunity to set the value bar high.

3. *Review the prospect's goals.* You can do this verbally or by presenting a list of goals in writing to the prospect. When doing this, you must be sure to show how your offering fits each of the prospect's decision criteria.

4. *Make sure to obtain reaction from your prospect throughout your presentation.* Asking questions such as "How would this improve your circumstances?" or "How would this help?" can accomplish this. If prospects do not talk, you do not know what they are thinking.

5. *Be ready to communicate all your unique strengths and how they meet your prospect's needs.* Answer the question, "Why are we the best choice?" before you make any presentation.

Making a Convincing Presentation

Selling is a *listen before you speak* business. You must speak in a clear, concise, specific, relevant, organized manner, and your ideas must flow smoothly so that prospects completely understand your explanations of products and services. What matters most is not what you say, but what the prospect understands from what you have said.

Few salespeople realize how difficult it actually is to explain something to someone. The average person has extreme difficulty putting together a dozen sentences in a way that make sense. The following points will help you develop your communication skills:

1. You must learn to think in an organized manner. Each idea should follow a logical sequence to create an understanding or mental image of the idea in your own mind.

2. In a successful sales situation, it is necessary for you to choose words that will convey the ideas from your mind into the prospect's mind in order to create the same understanding or mental image.

3. Sales aids can help improve the effectiveness of your communication—pictures, graphs, visuals, and recordings. You should constantly search and field-test anything that will improve your prospects' understanding of your product or service.

Choice of Words

*KISS—Keep It Simple Seller—*is an acronym that describes the tone of the sales presentation. Keeping it simple does not mean that you are condescending toward the prospect. Rather, it means that you strive to communicate clearly. It is not what you say that sells, but what the prospect understands of what you say. The prospect must be able to identify with your message in a meaningful way for real communication to take place. Short, simple words convey meanings best. The classic example is Abraham Lincoln's Gettysburg Address. It consists of 268 words, only 20 of which have three or more syllables. Only 52 words in the speech are two-syllable words, which means that 196 of the 268 words comprising one of the most famous speeches in the history of the United States are of one syllable.

You should choose words that are appropriate for your prospects based on their social style. When presenting to a purchasing agent who wants facts and figures, you might say, "Tests show that maintenance costs are 10 percent lower with our machine" or "Airfreight can save four full days." You might paint word pictures to the bakery owner that describe the scrumptious pastries and bread that can be prepared in a new high-capacity convection oven, along with discussing the oven's energy-efficiency ratings and the exact cost of buying on credit.

Using language appropriately includes using the terms of the trade. For example, "This thing here" does not communicate meaning as well as "induction coil." If you are in the printing business, you should know that "perfect binding" does not mean binding without a flaw, but rather binding with no stitching. But you also need to avoid the other extreme, as the use of technical language or jargon can confuse prospects and possibly lose them. A reference to "model number X34-J" may be no more meaningful to the customer than "This thing here." If you mean the induction coil, say so.

The point is not to impress the prospect, but rather to help the prospect understand. Focus on what prospects want to know, such as:

1. What are you offering me?
2. Exactly how does it work?
3. How will it help me?
4. Is it as good as you say it is? Who else says so?

5. What evidence can you offer that it is as good as you say?
6. Is it worth the price?
7. Will it help me accomplish what I really want to accomplish?

The words you use in sales presentations can trigger positive or negative emotions in prospects. Some words have strong emotional appeal and can be used very effectively in sales presentations, while other words should be avoided. Table 6.1 provides a short summary of words and phrases that should and should not be used in your sales presentations.

As a final comment on language, consider the following word choices and the impact they might have on a prospect:

- "cheaper" vs. "less expensive"
- "worthless" vs. "less value"
- "let me tell you" vs. "based on my experience"
- "it is in great condition" vs. "it has been well-cared for"
- "the latest thing" vs. "a breakthrough idea"
- "loud colors" vs. "bold look"
- "not difficult" vs. "it is easy"
- "I'm sorry" vs. "I apologize"
- "what we sell" vs. "what we offer"
- "strapped for cash" vs. "frugal times"
- "best" vs. "world class"
- "original" vs. "first of its kind"
- "knows all about it" vs. "has first-hand experience with"
- "down payment" vs. "initial investment"
- "listen to me" vs. "let's see what some customers say"
- "I think" vs. "here are some facts"

Components of a Successful Presentation

Prospects expect you to offer actionable and effective solutions. Listen to prospects carefully so you can align your solution with their needs and wants. When seeking to collaborate with prospects, involve them in the prescription for their problems. For example, you might say something like, "If we could . . . (suggest a course of action), how would that help?" The

TABLE 6.1 Choice of Words

Words That Bring Positive Responses

Truth (attracts immediate attention)		Excel	Stimulating	Relief

Truth (attracts immediate attention)   Excel   Stimulating   Relief
Let's (i.e., *let us*; implies togetherness)   Enormous   Health   Admired

Safe	Bargain	Beauty	Appetizing	Sociable
Fun	Stylish	Independent	Pride	Thinking
Value	Elegance	Tested	Modern	Low-cost
Time-saving	Necessary	Tasteful	Amibition	Espressive
Recommended	Growth	Home	Reputation	Up-to-date
Successful	Scientific	Mother	Economical	Hospitality
Efficient	Affectionate	Qualify	Warranty	Sympathy
Durable	Clean	Progress	Satus	Amusement
Personality	Popular	Guaranteed	Courtesy	Love
	Youth	Genuine		

Words to Avoid

I think	Cheap	Mistake	We try
Perhaps	Sometimes	Deal	Always
Maybe	I was wondering	I feel	Never
If	I might	I believe	Least expensive
Basically	I hope	Possibly	
Wrong	I just		

Phrases That Probe

What is your opinion?	What were the circumstances?	What happened then?
Why?	What do you think?	What do you consider?
Could you explain?	Can you help me?	Can you illustrate?
How do you feel about . . .?	What would you suggest?	How would you handle it?

Phrases That Irritate

You know?	You know what I mean?	Not really . . .	Old friend/pal!
Understand?	Like	Don't you know . . .?	No problem
Get the point?	You don't say?	I'll tell you what!	
See what I mean?	But honestly now!		

Nonwords

Uh	Um	Uh-hmm
Slang	Er	

prospect's response will help both you and the prospect understand that what he needs is an open dialogue.

As you and prospects work together to solve problems and co-create value, you must show a willingness to collaborate. You can do so with statements like, "Let's see how we might do that." Such a statement is, in essence, an invitation to the prospect to partner with you to seek a solution. It expresses your concern for the prospect's situation and is likely to get him more involved in the sales process.

Throughout the sales process, you must keep the following equation in mind:

$$V = Q/P$$
where
$$V = \text{Value, } Q = \text{Quality, and } P = \text{Price}$$

The value of a delivered product or service increases: (1) as the quality of that product or service increases; or (2) as the price of that product or service declines. In mathematical terms, if $Q = 8$ and $P = 2$, then $V = 4$ ($4 = 8/2$). However, as Q increases ($Q = 16$), V also increases ($8 = 16/2$), and so on.

As your dialogue with a prospect continues and you discuss various prescriptions, you can ask prospects questions like, "What would be the benefits to you if we took this approach?" or "What's important to you about . . . ?" The prospect's answers will help you understand what she values. As you and the prospect move closer to an acceptable solution, you can begin to develop the full prescription with statements such as, "Let's see if we can structure this solution so that it makes economic sense." At that point, you can begin to establish a price that is fair to both you and the prospect.

Drama

When choosing your words, you must help prospects visualize product/ service benefits by describing how things will be and how the prospect will feel after experiencing your prescribed solution. People think in both pictures and words; they seldom do anything without first visualizing themselves doing it successfully. By creating a postpurchase scenario for the prospect in which she is satisfied and her life is somehow made better by your product, you create a *drama*. You can say to her, "I can see you three months from now. By then your firm will have improved its handling of receivables. Your employees will be doing a super job, and will be saying that you made a great decision by purchasing this product."

Exaggeration

You should avoid exaggeration. Strong or exaggerated claims made in a sales presentation face one of two fates: the prospect will either discount them or attack them. Sharp prospects often pounce on your first exaggerated statement and, once they gain the offensive, will never let you off the hook. You cannot sell when you are on the defensive.

Promises

Robert Townsend, in *Up the Organization,* has provided some sound advice about promises:

> Keep them. If asked when you can deliver something, ask for time to think. Build a margin for safety. Name a date. Then deliver it earlier than you promised. The world is divided into two classes of people: the few who make good on their promises, and the many who don't. Get in column A and stay there. You'll be very valuable wherever you are.[1]

Salespeople cannot afford to be complacent about their relationships with customers. If they make promises, explicitly or implicitly, they must strive to keep them or risk losing the relationship.

Establishing Trust

As you choose your words, you must always consider the importance of establishing yourself as a trusted advisor. The prospect must be confident that you will not exploit his vulnerabilities. For salespeople, trust is like a nonquantifiable balance sheet asset. You must keep promises, sell value, create mutually beneficial prescriptions, and show that you truly want to serve customers well. The asset of trust appreciates in value as you continue to build relationships by offering fair-priced, high-quality, state-of-the-art products and services.

Suppose you say to a prospect, "Well, our delivery is not very good. The best we can do is six weeks." How will that prospect feel? Avoid being tempted to take sides with the prospect, adopting an attitude of "I'm with you, our company should do better." Such statements rarely gain prospect goodwill and never create prospect confidence. Instead, they destroy prospect confidence in you, your product, and your sales organization.

Sell Benefits, not Features

Prospects constantly ask themselves, "What's in it for me?" In answering this question, you must deal in facts. Avoid unsubstantiated claims and any confidence-destroying superlatives. Prospects often do not want products—they want the results of products. Every year, thousands upon thousands of drill bits are sold in the United States. Why? Do the purchasers want the drill bits, or do they want holes? You must sell results. You must sell prospects on what your products will do—not on what they are.

Features and Benefits

Most people know Robert Fulton invented the steamboat, but many do not realize he also invented the submarine. After he invented the submarine, he attempted to sell it to Napoleon. Fulton presented the idea to Napoleon by saying, "Sir, I have invented a boat that operates underwater. Last week I tested it in the Seine, and it submerged to a depth of 10 meters and sailed for 2 kilometers at a speed of 3 knots. It is operated by a hand-driven propeller and has a porthole so you can see underwater." Napoleon's reaction was, "Not interested!" Now, visualize what the results might have been if the conversation had gone something like this:

Fulton: Sir, do you desire to defeat the British army?

Napoleon: Yes.

Fulton: What is the one obstacle that prevents your invincible French army from smashing the British army on its own soil?

Napoleon: Well, the English Channel (and the British Navy), of course.

Fulton: Suppose I could provide you with a way to move your soldiers across the Channel in such a manner that the British could not see them until they reached the English coast? Would that be of interest to you?

Napoleon: Sold!

A feature is a desirable characteristic that is inherent in the performance of the product. Features are the technical aspects of the product—the materials used, the characteristics of those materials, how fast a product works, how much maintenance is required, size, shape, and so on. Product features are most likely to be tangible; they can be observed, felt, or experienced. A feature of a pencil, for example, might be its soft, fine-grained lead. An office copier might feature double-sided copying.

You must know the features of your products, but prospects always ask, "What will these features *do* for me?" To answer this question, you must be able to translate features into benefits. Sometimes you assume that the benefits are obvious, due to the outstanding features of a product, and that customers will automatically understand and appreciate these benefits. Customers, however, usually need you to explain and translate the results they can expect from all the product features.

Benefits are often intangible; they require explanation or interpretation to bring their merit and value into proper perspective for customers. A benefit is a definitive advantage, improvement, or satisfaction that a customer acquires or experiences from a feature of a product. A pencil with soft, fine-grained lead writes smoothly and distinctively; the result is a letter that is easy to read. Two-sided copying saves on paper costs, reduces mailing and handling costs, and lowers paper inventory requirements.

Product benefits lie at the heart of every sales presentation. To be effective, a presentation of benefits must focus on what makes them relevant to the specific prospect, because not all prospects are interested in the same benefits. You must emphasize how the product will meet the needs of the individual prospect. Salespeople who can identify a number of specific product benefits can work more competently with prospects than salespeople who can identify only a few general product benefits.

To expand your knowledge of the benefits of your products, create a features-benefits inventory, as illustrated in Chapter 3. Make a list of every significant product feature and relate each to a customer benefit. List all the features of the product, describe what each feature does, determine what benefits each one provides, and then develop a story around those benefits. A features-benefits inventory helps you organize the sales presentation around the customer, not the product. It provides a snapshot of those features and benefits that seem most relevant to certain customer groups.

Sales Presentation Structure

Structured sales presentations are presentations that salespeople memorize and use in all selling situations. The problem with structured sales presentations is that they presume there is one best way to sell. Prospects differ dramatically from one selling situation to the next. Although different firms have unique policies concerning how sales presentations should be prepared and what selling points should be stressed, presentations must be tailored to fit the needs of the prospect.

A sales presentation should make the prospect *want* the product or service being prescribed. Customize your presentations to show specific prospects how the prescribed product or service offering will fit their particular needs at that time. In order to accomplish this, your presentation must have the following four features:

1. *Completeness.* Be prepared to discuss every aspect of the product or service. This may not be necessary, but you must be ready if a prospect wants all the facts.
2. *Elimination of competition.* Your presentation must be perceived by the prospect as the best alternative to satisfy her need.
3. *Clarity.* Your presentation should leave no confusion in the prospect's mind.
4. *Prospect confidence.* You must make sure that the statements you make are true and that the interests of the prospect are paramount.

Demonstrations

The expression, "A picture is worth a thousand words," can be extended in sales to, "A demonstration is worth a thousand pictures." A demonstration can project a prospect into an emotional setting. Prospects like action, and most of them will remember results better than they will remember facts.

Make sure that demonstrations are part of your presentations. Demonstrations should be used to illustrate points that require more emphasis than can be given by words. They should *show* a product feature, how it works, and, above all, how the prospect benefits from it.

In short, demonstrations:

- Create conviction by showing prospects what your company's product/service can do, which is far more convincing than just telling them about it.

- Create a sense of ownership by getting prospects to examine or, even better, try out the product/service, since such hands-on involvement brings prospects close to the sensation of *owning* the product.
- Enable prospects to see for themselves what the product/service will do for them.
- Lead prospects to concentrate on what the product/service can *do* for them instead of what it will *cost.*
- Help set yourself and your products apart from the competition by *showing* how yours is "the best on the market for the prospect's situation."

When you cannot take a demonstration to prospects, you should try bringing prospects to the demonstration. For example, you might arrange for tours of your manufacturing facility and introduce your prospects to other key members of the sales team.

Dramatizing the Presentation

Showmanship is the skill of presenting something in an entertaining and dramatic manner. Most people would agree that a sales presentation should be interesting, visually striking, and forcefully effective. Showmanship, however, does not have to be complicated. It may consist of a simple display of product samples. Visual aids that are bold and colorful are very effective in introducing products to customers who are not familiar with them. Showmanship includes the enthusiasm transmitted by your voice. It does *not* include flamboyant attire or stunts that focus attention on you. The purpose of showmanship is to focus the prospect's attention on the performance of the product or service.

Dramatizing the sales presentation gets prospects more involved in it. Studies show that people often remember less than 10 percent of what they hear, but they remember 40 to 50 percent of what they both see and hear. If they also can be induced to touch, taste, or smell, they remember as much as 70 to 80 percent of the information presented. So you should think of creative ways to get and keep prospects involved in the sales presentation. Involvement leads to investment.

Catalogs

Nearly every sales organization has a catalog either in hard copy or on-line. Catalogs provide pictures of the product, descriptions of how it works, and information about various product features and their costs. The catalog is a basic sales tool, so you should be familiar with its contents—which products are included, where they are located, and what information is available in the catalog.

Sales catalogs range from being an effective sales supplement to being an absolute distraction. Catalogs that are poorly printed or formatted, dog-eared and sloppy, or hard to navigate online can actually distract from the sales presentation. In contrast, an effectively crafted catalog—perhaps showing the product in action, in color, and in a realistic situation—can be a great help.

Multimedia

Sales presentations are often augmented with multimedia presentation tools, the most common of which is Microsoft PowerPoint. Using a multimedia presentation tool can be a way to get your prospect's attention and make your presentations memorable. The multimedia aspect of your presentation should serve as an enhancement to the information that you are presenting. Multimedia presentations can be given in person or, increasingly, by way of online delivery mechanisms, such as videoconferencing and webinars.

Persuading Prospects to Buy What Is Prescribed

Communication between you and prospects is multifaceted. Here are a few of the more challenging communication problems salespeople face: (1) fear appeals; (2) discontent; (3) empathy; (4) presumptions; (5) graciousness; and (6) specificity.

Fear Appeals

Many prospects are inclined to say things like "I need to think it over" or "I'll have to discuss this with the other members of the buying team." One approach to energize prospects toward a purchase and a relationship involves the use of fear. You can paint a positive picture using fear by describing the consequences of *not* buying. For example, when a seller was confronted with a situation in which a buyer demonstrated fear of making a decision, she immediately pulled out a calculator. Asked by the prospect what she was doing, she replied, "I'm calculating how much revenue your firm will lose by delaying your decision for two weeks." Such a statement puts pressure on the prospect, and generally high-pressure closing tactics are not recommended. If you are dealing with facts, however, and the prospect has assessed the situation and agreed that your prescription provides value, you cannot afford to leave the prescription on the table without some kind of decision. This is a difficult strategy to employ; but when it is used appropriately, fear can be a healthy motive. Fear is a strong motivating factor in human behavior.[2] Financial and social insecurity are powerful buying motives that stimulate people to buy many things they might otherwise get along without. What's more powerful than learning your competition is doing something to gain a competitive advantage.

Discontent

Another strong factor that can work for you is the ability to make people less happy with their current condition. This does not mean that you should use questionable tactics to create discontent, but prospects often are content simply because they are complacent or unaware of the availability of superior alternatives. Therefore, you can create discontent by raising the prospect's awareness. New ways of looking at a product or situation can create discontent as prospects recognize that they should be dissatisfied with what they have or with what they are doing. You can often help a prospect see things in a new light.

You can encourage a prospect to reevaluate current conditions. First, you must create a new standard for judging the situation—a standard that is different from the one the prospect is using. For example, a prospect's current standard may be "savings." A new proposal may not be able to show impressive savings, but it may be able to offer a new standard, such as "broader market coverage," that might lead the prospect to become discontented with her firm's present situation and consider a change in suppliers—not on the basis of savings, but for broader market coverage.

Second, you must ensure that the prospect adopts the new standard as her own. A new standard must be thought-provoking enough to lead the prospect to view her present situation in a new light. What may have measured up before is no longer considered adequate. Thus, she becomes unhappy with the present way of doing things. The prospect has a problem, and you have a solution.

A prospect who thinks that $10,000 is a lot of money to spend on a particular type of product or service will probably not be interested in what any salesperson has to say about a product at that price point. The prospect sees the cost of $10,000 as being too expensive and thinks the money could be better spent elsewhere. You must help this prospect see the situation in a new light. For example, one method used by successful advertising salespeople is to show the prospect how she can use $10,000 to secure one or two new customers who will more than pay for the advertising expenditure.

As an analogy, when people are in good health, they do not want medicine. When they get seriously ill, however, they want it badly. This is because their illness has made them aware of a need. So it is with prospects. You must help them become aware of a particular lack, want, or need—and then be ready to prescribe a cure. Here is where you must think of both the short term and the long term. A popular lyric from the movie *Mary Poppins* suggests, "Just a spoonful of sugar helps the medicine go down." When you make learning a part of the buying and selling experience, you can create a positive experience for the prospect. Salespeople who want prospects to learn will take their time and nurture the learning process as they proceed to the completion of their presentations. In the long-term, prospect understanding and learning are critical for the partnership to continue. This is true even after a sale is made.

You can use electronic media to send information in small, easy-to-learn doses. For example, immediately after concluding a presentation, you can send the prospect an email thanking him for his time and providing some added information of value, either to reinforce the decision of a prospect who has decided to buy or to help persuade one who has not made a decision. Consider this strategy versus the practice of loading up prospects with huge notebooks and manuals. Parceling out the information by providing periodic learning material makes it much easier for the prospect to learn and reduces the risk that he will feel overwhelmed.

Empathy

When you are able to empathize with prospects, you have laid the ground-work for providing an intelligent answer to the prospect's problem. As Dr. Herbert M. Greenberg says:

> Empathy is the ability to relate to people—to feel as the other guy feels, to put yourself in the other fellow's shoes. This quality, which allows you to perceive intuitively the thoughts and emotions of others, is strong in all men who live by swaying opinion. In selling, it is empathy, which allows you to establish psychological feedback between you and your prospect, or your customer, in order to discover what arguments will appeal to him—often before he knows them himself.[3]

Empathy is about realizing that if you are to sell what your prospect buys, then you must sell through your prospect's eyes.

You must answer this question in the mind of the prospect: "What's in it for me?" You can do this by: (1) explaining to the prospect that you have examined his situation; (2) demonstrating that you do understand that situation; (3) proving that you know what he wants; and (4) working with the prospect to convince him that you have a prescription to help answer his problem.

You must be patient and let prospects consider statements thoughtfully. You must let them realize that you know the answer. If used for the purpose of demonstrating patience with prospects as they make decisions, silence can be very effective for inviting prospect confidence. The prospect knows that you recognize his problem because you have just stated it. And once he offers confidences, you have confirmation of what his problem is.

Presumptions

One direct way for you to demonstrate that you can prescribe a solution to a prospect's problem is to say, "It would be presumptuous of me to tell you that you will get the same results that Ms. Pommier got, but it wouldn't have to be *that* good to be worth talking about." What are you attempting to do here? You are naming a satisfied customer, a third party, and letting that third party help you tell your prospect how your prescribed solutions have assisted another customer. As you work with the new prospect, telling her what can be done about her situation, your prescription becomes more believable because it has already worked for another prospect in a similar situation. This is a gracious way to make a point.

Statements such as "It would be presumptuous of me to tell you," "I'd be taking too much for granted," or "I can't guarantee you that" are good shock absorbers. They build believability. You may, in fact, not know for sure what the prospect's problem is. If this is the case, you may presume too much if you state emphatically that she can get "X percentage" of savings or increased coverage. However, you can introduce the idea that the prospect should reasonably be able to expect a given result because that has been the experience reported by other satisfied customers. In this way, you achieve credibility. The prospect makes the association and thinks, "Well, if *she* got that much, then I ought to get pretty close to that."

Specificity

You should be specific by naming dates, places, and people. This adds to the validity of your statements. For example, you might say, "Mr. Lamar of the Ajax Company wrote us this letter dated August 30th and told us," and then show the prospect the letter. The phrase "Mr. Lamar . . . told us" allows the existing customer to say things with more credibility than you might be able to do. This kind of statement is much stronger than saying, "I saved Mr. Lamar . . ." or "We saved Mr. Lamar . . ." In order for such endorsements to work effectively, however, they must contain *specifics*. The endorsing customer has spent a specific amount of time, a specific amount of money, and a specific amount of energy, and he is satisfied with a specific set of results received from your product or service.

Prospects and customers have explicit expectations about their interactions with you. When you meet those expectations, the prospects and customers can be satisfied or even delighted. You must remember that needs and expectations shape prospect behavior. The desired outcome with regard to prospects' expectations is for the prospect to get what is anticipated from a sales prescription. Failing to meet expectations creates prospect disappointment.

Prospects have expectations that their personal needs (e.g., to be fairly treated, to maintain one's image) as well as their professional needs will be met. They also have expectations that the product or service will be reliable.

Needs focus on the prospect; *expectations* focus on product or service performance.

Moving toward Purchase

In the purchase stage, the focus of a sales presentation shifts from presenting product benefits to encouraging the prospect to make a buying commitment. Frequently, the conversation turns to discussing such things as the terms of the sale. Typical comments made by you at this stage might be: "The price is only $840.00 dollars per lot," or "Our installation crew can be at your plant first thing Monday morning," or "We had better get started processing the loan application papers."

At this point, you summarize the benefits and then move to the trial close. When summarizing benefits, you may find it useful to help a prospect visualize how projected results can improve her situation. You also can present the terms of the sale in such a way that the benefits are maximized and the costs are minimized.

The Trial Close

You can check or test the prospect's attitude toward buying—the degree or extent to which the prospect is prepared to make a decision to buy or not to buy—by using the trial close technique. Trial closing is like taking the temperature of the buyer's interest to check whether he is hot or cold on buying what you are selling.

Checking the Prospect's Temperature

A temperature question is phrased to require an answer from the prospect that will reveal the degree or extent of his willingness to buy. The temperature question (or trial close) is not a *closing* question because you are not asking the prospect to make a decision to buy. If you ask for a buying decision before the prospect or customer is psychologically ready, you run the risk of losing the sale and the relationship, as the prospect may perceive that you are pressuring him to buy. The great value of the temperature question technique is that it gradually leads the prospect's mind from the realm of opinions to the actual moment of decision with a minimum of stress, strain, and anxiety. You should remember to avoid asking questions that can be answered with a yes or a no. Here are two examples of temperature questions:

- What is your opinion of the plan we've discussed?
- How would you pay for this service if you bought today?

Then, ask for a decision.

Gauging Customer Reactions

During the course of any sales interaction, a prospect's readiness to buy fluctuates from high to low levels. You should be alert to states of "high readiness" indicated by customer reactions. A *reaction* is anything the prospect says or does that indicates whether the prospect agrees or disagrees with you. It is a visible or outward indication of an inward mental attitude. You should familiarize yourself with the concepts of verbal and nonverbal clues covered in Chapter 5 to become adept at handling customer reactions.

Many people can control their overt actions, but most people cannot control their involuntary reactions to various stimuli that affect their basic instincts. Prospect attitudes will reveal themselves. A key issue for you is developing the ability to identify a buying attitude. Prospects may not realize that they are reacting to what is being said or done, but those reactions are indications that tell you how or in what direction to proceed in the sales interview. You must be able to recognize and classify the meaning of prospect reactions.

The prospect's attitude on any given point may be affirmative, indifferent, or negative; the prospect's overall reactions will indicate how she feels. Reactions can be placed in two categories, positive and negative, and are expressed in two ways, physically and/or verbally. Examples of some verbal prospect reactions are provided in Table 6.2.

A prospect's positive reaction can come at any point in the sales call. However, positive reactions toward the latter part of the sales call are generally more valuable because the prospect has more facts and information on which to base a logical and lasting decision.

Your responsibility is to make it easy for a prospect to make a decision.

Traditionally, it has been recommended that salespeople employ trial closes to trigger a reaction that will definitely reveal the prospect's buying attitude and lead him to a decision, either positive or negative.

TABLE 6.2 Gauging Customer Reactions

Physical

Positive	Negative
Smile	Frown
Laugh	Clenched hands
Affirmative nod	Tense manner
Relaxed manner	Indifference
Interested manner	Surliness
	Shakes head
	Bored manner
	Too polite
	Looks at watch or clock

Verbal

Positive	Negative
Agrees with what you say	Refuses to talk
Talks freely	Finds fault or criticizes
Gives personal or confidential information	Makes excuses
	An "objection" of any kind

Positive Verbal Prospect Reactions

- If I authorize purchase of this office equipment, when could we expect delivery?
- What are your payment terms? I would need to know these before I agree to make a purchase.
- What quantity discounts does your firm offer?
- Am I correct in stating that your maintenance contract is valid for three years?
- This product appears to fit my firm's needs very well.
- Perhaps this equipment would help reduce my firm's maintenance costs.

Sample Closing Signals

- The prospect relaxes, particularly if the prospect assumes a pleased and relaxed expression after having been cool and argumentative.
- The prospect reexamines the model or sample of your product after you have finished discussing it.
- The prospect picks up sales literature of your offering and reexamines some of the pages that have descriptions of features with which she seems pleased.

(continued)

TABLE 6.2 Gauging Customer Reactions (*continued*)

- The prospect asks you to confirm your shipment or other terms of sale.
- The prospect compares the details of your offering with those of a competitor.
- The prospect appears pleased and nods in agreement, as you outline all the benefits of your product or service in your presentation.
- You have finished your demonstration and the prospect appears pleased with it.
- The prospect asks for your *opinion*—not necessarily more product or service information.

    You should take any of these closing signals as a sign to ask for the order.

Source: Adapted from Impact Sales Training Company, "Zing! Using Technology to Enhance Sales Presentations" (2001). http://www.makinganimpact.com/newsletters/nwsltr-usingtech.html.

7 Conviction and Motivation

A man always has two reasons for doing anything; a good reason and the
real reason.

> —John Pierpont Morgan

The Conviction and Motivation Steps

A t this point, you face the moment of truth. The prospect has lis-
tened to your entire presentation and has heard your prescribed
solution. Everything seems to be right—until the prospect wants
to "think about it" or "check out a couple of other sources first" or "wait
until the new budgets are out." Possibly, though he will not admit it, the
prospect is distracted by personal reasons and just not in the mood to make
a decision.

Unless the prospect is "closed" at this point (i.e., he has committed to
buying the product), you can expect him to raise questions (objections).
Therefore, you still have some crucial tasks to perform. You must *convince*
your prospect of the validity and desirability of your offer and *motivate*
him toward *completing the transaction*. This chapter is about how to persuade the prospect that a real problem exists and that you have the best solution to it.

The purpose of the conviction and motivation steps is to convince the
prospect that your organization and product/service have the best value
and will satisfy the prospect's desires in the long term. Once conviction has
registered (i.e., when you have overcome all objections and answered all
questions), you seek to motivate the prospect to take the appropriate buying action.

Conviction Conveys Value

While you have been prescribing a solution to the prospect's problem, the
prospect has been thinking, "Is the product really that good?" Now, you

must answer this question in a straightforward, simple manner. Unless you can convince prospects that your solutions are best for them, and unless prospects can understand the product or service to their satisfaction, you will not make many sales. Keep this thought in mind that prospects seldom buy what they do not understand. For example, suppose you sell batteries and your company has perfected a process in which the life of its battery is 30 percent longer than that of competitors. When you describe this feature, customers can understand it and it is measurable. Conviction may require the use of industry standards created by experts. Alternatively, a report from an independent agency such as *Consumer Reports* or a government agency such as the Federal Trade Commission can also provide proof of value. The key is that prospects may want you to prove the validity of your assertions about the product and about the standards of measurement that you are presenting.

The objective of the conviction step is to build on your prescription by further explaining aspects of your offering that either have already been discussed or were not covered in your initial prescription. The purpose, use, features, and benefits of the product or service must be explained so clearly and logically that the prospect completely understands, accepts, and believes what you say. Only by selling value can you be convincing.

Components of Customer-Perceived Value

What is the source of customer-perceived value? Does value derive from the product, the brand image, the sales firm, or you? Is the prospect's value of your product/service objectively defined or perceived? Answers to such questions present knowledge problems for you. To be effective in the conviction stage of the sales process, you must embrace the idea that prospects will not buy if they do not perceive value.

Value for a prospect can come in a variety of forms. As shown in Table 7.1, products hold both economic and noneconomic value for prospects.[1]

Economic value relates to things such as performance and price. Noneconomic value relates to things such as brand and packaging. Further, the extrinsic value of the product is the value that you bring in terms of support and service. Intrinsic value is the value that the prospect derives directly from the product itself. At this stage of the sales process, you endeavor to ensure that the prospect completely understands the *total* value you are offering.

TABLE 7.1 Components of Prospect Value

	Economic	Noneconomic
Intrinsic (Product)	Performance	Brand name
	Reliability	Styling
	Technology	Packaging
	Price	Appearance
	Maintenance	
	Durability	
Extrinsic (Seller)	Operator training	Reputation
	Maintenance training	Reliability
	Warranty	Responsiveness
	Parts availability	Salesperson relationship
	Post-purchase costs	Service

Source: Adapted from N. Tzokas and M. Saren, "Value Transformation in Relationship Marketing" (2000), http://www.ebusinessforum.gr/old/content/downloads/ap0005.pdf.

Value considered in the context of relationships is difficult to measure. One way to assess relationship value is to calculate customer-perceived value:

$$\text{Customer-perceived value} = \frac{\text{Core solution} + \text{Value Added} + \text{Value of Relationship}}{\text{Price} + \text{Cost of Relationship}}$$

Notice that total customer-perceived value is a function of the total benefits divided by the total cost of purchasing. Your job is to convey the total value in such a way that the prospect sees the big picture. The prospect is not just buying a tangible product; she is buying a *total package* of goods and services at a price that is small in relation to the total benefits.

Competitive Advantage

You must know your competitors' offerings and know how your own offerings compare to them. This knowledge will allow you to manage comparisons brought up by prospects during your presentation and to determine where your offering has advantages from the customer's perspective. Remember, it is what the customer thinks, not what you think. An advantage is an aspect of your offering that is superior to that of a competitive offering. If a prospect is considering the purchase of Cisco's blade servers, the simple and fast deployment feature provides benefits to the customer. However, simple and fast deployment would represent an advantage only if the prospect considers Cisco's blade deployment time superior to that of a competitor like Hewlett-Packard. Without criticizing the competition, you should remain professional in pointing out and validating the unique differences in your product or service as compared to that of the competition.

Role of Product Knowledge and Self-Knowledge

Most customers do business with multiple suppliers. Ideally, you must provide enough knowledge and value to the prospect to convince him to do business with you exclusively. Prospects who are convinced can become loyal customers.

Product knowledge precedes professional proficiencies. When you know your products and are personally convinced of their value, you improve your self-confidence and enthusiasm. Consider the following questions in preparing to demonstrate to prospects your product knowledge and knowledge of how your products are superior to those of the competition:

- Precisely what do I have to offer to prospects?
- Specifically, how many different types of help am I offering to them?
- What services do I have to offer that are better than those of the competition?
- Who says or agrees that these services are better, and why?

One way to prepare for managing competitive information is to assume a prospect has asked you to answer the following question in twenty-five words or less: "Why should I buy from you instead of your competition?"

You need to ask yourself: What unique or exclusive benefit (advantage) do I have to offer to my prospect? At least one unique benefit always exists—you yourself. Your knowledge of the business, application of that knowledge to the prospect's particular problem, and personal attention and follow-through are exclusive benefits you can offer to prospects. The prospect cannot get these things from anyone but you. You should sell yourself to prospects by assuring that they will be getting an exclusive benefit at no extra cost—namely, your personal commitment to the relationship.

You can also refer to your satisfied customer surveys to determine why your satisfied customers do business with you. Check to see whether any of these reasons would be important to particular prospects. Opinions of other customers and their faith in you may help prospects feel more comfortable because these testimonials demonstrate that you and the sales company are "tried and true."

The questions shown in Table 7.2 represent a "knowledge plan" for you. Knowledge management entails acquisition, maintenance, and dissemination. In order to build prospect conviction, you must understand how customers use products, how you can increase value to prospects, how prospects measure success, and what might occur to change a prospect's use of a product.

TABLE 7.2 Knowledge Checklist: Building Conviction

Customer/Product Interactions	• Why do customers use our product/service?
	• How can this prospect use our product/service?
	• What prospect challenges does our product/service solve?
	• What additional or new challenges does our product/service create?
	• How could our product/service be easier for the prospect to use?
	• How can services be expanded to reduce prospect/customer challenges?
Customer Values	• How does the prospect define success?
	• How can we make this prospect more successful?
	• What does the prospect see as its distinctive competence?
	• What are this prospect's challenges?
	• What does this customer value?
	• What changes does this prospect see in the environment?
Prospect Relationships	• How does this prospect make purchasing decisions?
	• What must we do to increase our percentage of the customer's budget?
	• How do we compare to our competition?
	• What does this prospect see as our distinctive competence?
	• Under what circumstances might we lose this customer?
	• How much of the total purchasing budget does the customer spend with us?

Gaining Conviction

To successfully navigate the conviction step, you need to clearly, logically, and truthfully present your solutions to prospects' problems. In presenting a solution, you should be sure to:

1. Explain what the product or service is and how it works.
2. Explain the facts and features (selling points) of the product/service and their related benefits so the prospect can understand the benefit or value to him.
3. Establish the prospect's belief in you and what you say by presenting *evidence* (e.g., testimonials from satisfied customers and/or articles from the newspaper or other media) that supports or substantiates the facts and features of your product/service.
4. Explain any *related information* that the prospect would like to know (e.g., facts about the sales company, industry, or locality).

Complicated products and services require more detailed explanation than simple ones, but regardless of the complexity or simplicity of the product/service, you should be able to give a fairly short, clear definition of your product/service that the prospect can understand. Here's an example:

> Mr. D'Agostino, this workforce optimization plan is simply a contractual agreement between you and our company that states that our company assumes responsibility for your company's human resources and personnel services. You will be relieved of time-consuming duties, gaining the freedom to focus on the aspects of your business that are most important to you.

Providing Evidence

When you present relevant and current evidence about the facts, features, and benefits of your products/services, you will convince prospects that you are telling the truth. You are engaging in the role of trusted advisor. Prospects want to believe you, but they must have a reason to believe. *Documentation beats speculation!* A good rule for you to follow is this: You should never tell a prospect anything about a product or service unless that claim can be supported with evidence.

In providing evidence to prospects, you should provide only enough information to establish the prospect's belief in you without overwhelming the prospect. You don't have to provide the same type of or amount of evidence to each prospect. Following is an example of using just enough evidence to make a convincing case:

> Mr. Hanson, you don't have to worry about whether your customers will buy this product, because we have a money-back guarantee [feature]. You see, the contract specifically mentions our guarantee [evidence], which means [linking phrase] that you can buy with confidence [benefit]. Another wonderful feature is the call center support that my company offers [feature]. Notice the toll-free number provided for your customers [evidence], which means that [linking phrase] should they have any questions about using the product, they can contact our call center free of charge. This removes the burden of your having to answer all product-related questions [benefit].

To summarize, you should be as concerned about your knowledge and skill in presenting factual information as you are about the actual facts surrounding the product or service. You should list the relevant facts together with evidence supporting those facts. Ultimately, your goal is to use this information to secure the prospect's agreement that you are offering something of value.

Structuring a Complete Unit of Conviction

Now all the components of a complete unit of conviction can be put together in a selling situation. But first, the following definitions of terms will help you understand how they are being used:

- *Fact.* According to *Webster's* dictionary, a fact is "the truth, the case, a reality"; it is an indisputable, self-evident point about the product or service.
- *Claim.* A claim is "that which is stated as a fact." This is a feature or selling point of the product or service. Although claims might not be true in every case, they have been true in so many cases that you feel justified in stating them as fact.
- *Wild claim.* This sort of claim is a lie. You must not use wild claims, as it is wrong for you to misrepresent your products or services. The

products or services you sell are either good enough so that you do not have to lie about them, or you should not be selling them. Salespeople who lie are usually those who are too lazy to learn the real truth and value of their product or service, or those who are strongly uneducated about professional selling.

- *Benefit.* A benefit is the end result of the particular fact, feature, or selling point, or what the fact or feature means to the prospect. Again, every prospect wants to know: "What is in it for me? What am I really getting for my money?" Every time you state a fact or feature and its *related benefit,* you reinforce the point that the prospect will get his money's worth. You are selling value instead of low prices, deals, or discounts.
- *Linking phrase.* This is a short phrase (such as "which means to you") that ties the *fact or feature,* the *evidence,* and the *related benefit* together smoothly and in an orderly manner. It focuses or directs the prospect's mind from one idea to a related idea in a natural, logical sequence.

The following demonstrates the conviction step in action, using a data security software installation as an example.

Step 1: State Fact or Feature

First, state facts and features. For example:

Mr. Maple this complete data security plan includes a legal contract between your company and ours that states that our company will pay your company a specified amount in dollars if someone hacks into your company's database and steals data. This is guaranteed, and my company can never cancel this contract as long as the monthly payment requirement is met.

Step 2: Offer Evidence to Document Fact or Feature

Next, offer evidence to document the facts and features. For example, you might say, "Look at what Company X said about our service" and then present the following testimonial letter:

Dear Mr. Salesperson:

Data security is a big issue at my company. We store highly sensitive and confidential information that, if leaked, would give our competitors data they could use to put us out of business. The complete data security plan that we bought gives us peace of mind, enabling us to focus on our business.

Sincerely,

Ean Emile

You would then follow up with a comment like, "Mr. Maple, I'm sure you can appreciate the value of such data security. How safe is your company's data now?"

Step 3: Show Related Buyer Benefits with "Which Means to You"

You should memorize this sequence and make it part of every presentation: fact or feature, evidence, linking phrase, and benefit. Notice in the following example how the salesperson uses this format and presents company statistics to support his claims:

> Now, you can see what an excellent plan this is and how it will serve your particular need. I'm also including software upgrades in this plan for a few extra cents per month [feature]. This will ensure that your computer system stays protected [benefit].
>
> Mr. Maple, according to the latest information from *Trade World* magazine, our company is currently protecting 60 percent of the companies in your industry [evidence]. So you can see how valuable this service is, which means that your company can join others that have experienced the same issues that you have [linking phrase]. Our company, after a six-month period, will review our installation and give you a complete report of the number of hackers that tried to get into your database [benefit].
>
> Mr. Maple, our company has been in business for 15 years and has district offices in 30 states [facts]. [The salesperson presents a territory map.] Here is a map showing our office locations [evidence]. Now, this means that regardless of where your company's offices are located, we can help [linking phrase]. We will be able to have personal contact with your managers and ensure that your program is kept in order and up-to-date [benefit].

Step 4: Secure Agreement with a Wrap-Up Question

The wrap-up question is where you get the prospect to agree that this fact, this evidence, and this buyer's benefit are all important to him. How do you do this? You simply ask, "How important is this to you?" In this step, first ask a wrap-up question such as: "Mr. Maple, as you have seen, this complete data security package will guarantee that you will have peace of mind so you can concentrate on your business. You will feel better knowing this has been taken care of. . . . How does this sound?" [trial close] If the prospect agrees, move immediately into the closing question: "With your permission, I'd like to go ahead and take care of this for you now."

Handling Objections

Handling objections is an important aspect of conviction and motivation. No matter how prepared you are, the prospect/customer will have questions and/or concerns that you must address. Objections come in many forms; some are genuine concerns, and some are just excuses for not wanting to commit at the moment. Effective salespeople can anticipate objections, answer them with confidence, probe for more concerns, and quickly get back to motivating the prospect/customer to make a favorable decision. It is important to remember that professional salespeople stay calm and composed while listening to objections, and answer the prospect's questions and concerns with conviction.

Anticipating Objections

Agile salespeople anticipate prospects' objections and prepare answers before making sales calls. Prospects will ask questions about how the technical aspects of the product/service solution can help prevent the occurrence of problems. You must anticipate value improvements. Value improvements can be anything that will help prospects see that their overall situation can be improved through the purchase of your product or service, and they can originate from any of the four values—economic, noneconomic, intrinsic, extrinsic—described earlier. Informative sales calls show that you have done your homework, understand the prospect's situation, and have given thought to the prospect's concerns. Such preparation can also be powerful in relationship building.

Types of Objections

Prospects and customers may raise objections at any time during a sales presentation. Three common types of objections are *stoppers, stalls,* and *searches.*

Stoppers are genuine objections to all or part of your proposal. The prospect may say that he does not have the money, is not authorized to purchase, or does not want the product or service. If this is true, clearly you have made a prospecting mistake, or the prospect's situation has changed. Maybe your estimate of the prospect's ability to pay was too high. Perhaps you did not ask for a sales appointment with the right person, or perhaps you overestimated the prospect's desire. Review the MAD principle discussed in Chapter 3 and examine the qualifiers discussed there. Prospects must have the *money, authority,* and the *desire* to purchase. You must ask enough questions to determine if this objection is genuine or just an excuse. Almost any objection sounds like a genuine refusal at first; however, underneath an objection may be a stall or a request for additional information.

Stalls, in contrast to stoppers, are invalid objections (i.e., excuses). The prospect is really saying, "You haven't convinced me that my need is strong enough for me to do something about it today." Following are some examples of stalls:

- "I have another appointment in a few minutes. Just leave your information, and I'll get back to you."
- "This is my slow season. Come back in the fall."
- "I'll need to talk this over with our buying committee."

When handling stalls, remember that it is human nature to resist change, and many prospects perceive you as someone who wants to make them change.

Searches are requests for more information—either from you, the competition, or both. Examples of searches are:

- "I'm just shopping right now."
- "We're early in the buying process. I need to visit with other vendors, and I'll get back to you."
- "Your competition is offering a lower price."

The list of examples of stoppers, stalls, and searches could go on indefinitely. It is important for you to know how to handle such objections. Keep in mind that prospects are busy, and busy people ignore unsolicited communications. Even when you have progressed through several presentations, a prospect may still not be very responsive. Keep in mind that "hot buttons" open doors. Tell prospects exactly how you can help them and make sure you can justify your value, as prospects can purchase anything they want or not purchase anything at all.

Overcoming Objections

Learn to welcome objections. When a prospect raises objections, it can mean that she is interested but is trying to reconcile the expense of purchasing. Objections indicate that you are just that much closer to completing the transaction. You should remain positive in your attitude, gain a better understanding of the objection, and answer the concern based on the classification of the objection.

As a general rule of thumb, your formula for handling objections has five parts:

1. *Listen* very carefully to the prospect's objection.
2. *Clarify* the concern.
3. *Cushion* the objection.
4. *Classify* the objection to determine when and how to answer it.
5. *Answer* the objection with concern, conviction, and enthusiasm.

Listening, Clarifying, and Cushioning the Objection

Before answering an objection, hear the prospect out. Let prospects speak and encourage them to voice all their concerns and complaints (i.e., objections). You should not interrupt prospects; they need the opportunity to express themselves completely. Next, you should clarify your understanding of prospects' concerns, using phrases such as: "Let me make sure I understand . . ." and "So, what you're saying is . . ." Then use "shock absorbers" to cushion the answers to the objections.

A shock absorber (or *cushion*) is a statement acknowledging the prospect's objections. It indicates to the prospect that you understand and appreciate the prospect's feelings and perspective. Cushions should always demonstrate a sincere agreement with the prospect on some point. Following are some examples of cushions:

- *"I know exactly how you feel, Mrs. York."* Others have felt the same way when they first heard about this product. It's interesting, though, that after using the product, they became enthusiastic about it. In fact, here's a letter from someone who had the same feelings that you're expressing now."
- *"That's certainly a logical concern, Ms. Albert."* You want to be sure that you're getting the best value for the money. Let's review these quality specifications, and perhaps you will see why my product is slightly more expensive than my competitors' products."
- *"I can certainly appreciate why you think that way, Ms. Williams."* Many of my best clients thought that way at first. Let's see if I can do a better job of explaining why the contract terms are spelled out that way."

Notice that the first thing you do is acknowledge the concern. This diffuses the situation so that prospects do not feel like their concerns are being trivialized. Prospects' concerns are never trivial—they are very important.

Classifying the Objection

Before you can effectively answer an objection, you must thoroughly understand what kind of objection it is and when it should be answered. If the objection is a true stopper (i.e., a legitimate issue), there is little for you to do but terminate the presentation as quickly and gracefully as possible. You should be professional and, perhaps, ask for a referral. However, if the objection merely *sounds* like a stopper but really is not (something that would be revealed through more questioning), you must overcome the objection.

If the objection is a stall, you need to reengage your prospect/customer. To deal with a stall you can say something like the following:

- "Ms. Folse, if now is not a good time for you, when is a better time? I can come back this afternoon at 2:00, or would tomorrow morning at 8:30 be better?"
- "I can understand that the buying committee needs to be involved in this decision. Tell me, Mr. Watson, which aspects of my proposal do you think the committee members will like, and which ones do you think they won't like?"
- "Dr. Burns, with the semester resuming in a few months, I am sure that you will be even busier in the fall than you are now. Perhaps today we can agree to ship the books in July. That way, you'll feel confident that your books will be in the bookstore in time for the new semester. All I need is authorization from you, and we won't have to schedule another appointment to go back through this presentation."
- "Mr. Oliver, after looking at how much profit you could make selling this product, are you sure you want to wait?"

Many times, prospects' objections are not really objections at all, but rather requests for more information. For example:

- "I can't afford it" may really mean "Tell me more about your extended payment plan."
- "The equipment sure seems flimsy" may be a way of asking, "What evidence can you offer me to ensure that your product is sturdy and reliable?"
- "I am satisfied with my present vendor" may actually mean "I really haven't thought much about switching suppliers. Why should I spend time thinking about it now?"

Answering the Objection

Once you have gained a better understanding of an objection and have classified it, you are in a position to answer it. Following are five classic methods. Notice that the word *but* does not appear in these statements. You should avoid using this word because it makes your statements sound argumentative.

1. *Forestall the objection.* Salespeople who have handled a particular objection many times can build an answer to that objection into their presentations. For example, if you know that your product is priced higher than competitors' products, say this up-front: "Mr. Laten, as you'll see, our product is priced higher than my competitors' products. This is because we use a higher grade of steel for the chassis."

2. *Compensate.* No product is perfect. Buyers know that products have strengths and weaknesses. A product that is superior on all dimensions would be very expensive. If a prospect identifies a real weakness in the product, your best option is to admit it and emphasize the product's compensating strengths. For example, you might say, "Yes, I know our price is higher; that's because our product is guaranteed for three years instead of one."

3. *Counter.* This method allows you to discuss additional selling points and to present an opposing viewpoint without becoming argumentative. For example, "I understand how you feel; perhaps we can look at it this way."

4. *Boomerang.* Sometimes you will encounter an objection that can be turned into a *reason for buying.* Suppose, for example, that the prospect says, "My business is too small to purchase smartphones for all our salespeople." You may be able to turn that objection into a reason for buying by saying, "Ms. Myles, *that's the very reason you should buy.* You have five salespeople who are trying to manage their time better. The smartphones will increase their time efficiency and your profits while not taking a big bite out of your budget. Five smartphones will cost only . . ."

5. *Feel, felt, found.* Prospects can become emotional as they raise objections. When encountering emotional situations, you can use the classic "feel, felt, found" method of overcoming objections. If the prospect says, "This software program is very expensive; I'm not sure I want to spend so much money on data protection," you can respond, "Mr. Coale, I can understand how you *feel* about the price. Many of my customers *felt* the same way until they *found* that the peace of mind that came with the purchase of the best data protection software on the market is priceless."

Negotiation

After you have answered all the prospect's objections and concerns and have achieved conviction, many times you need to negotiate the terms of the offer. Generally, if you have to negotiate, you have not convinced the prospect/customer that the offer has enough value. When you do have to negotiate terms, however, you want the results of your efforts to be such that both you and your prospects get a good deal. Thus, win-win negotiating is the rule.

Creating a Win-Win Outcome

To create a win-win outcome, both buyers and sellers have to be willing to make concessions (i.e., to give up something). The sketch in Figure 7.1 illustrates this idea. It depicts four automobiles arriving at the same time at an intersection with a malfunctioning traffic light. Each automobile is unable to progress because it is blocked by another. The simple solution would be for one of the cars to allow another to pass; then everyone could pass. Each driver, however, may be unwilling to be the first to do it. The drivers might instead lean on their horns and shout a few choice words at one an-

FIGURE 7.1 The Stalemate

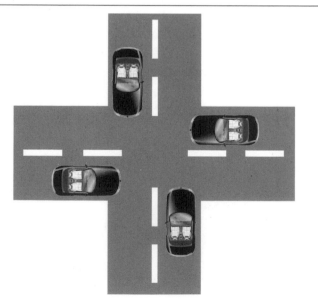

other. This cartoon illustrates a common human failing: We often sacrifice a major interest because we refuse to give up on a minor one. How many sales have you lost because you would not concede on minor issues?

In negotiating with prospects with opposing viewpoints, do not lose sight of your ultimate objectives: to sell a product to satisfy prospect needs and to build long-lasting business relationships, which will generate more business for you in the long run. Search for a compromise—a common ground. The best negotiators in selling realize this. They know there is virtually no limit to the kinds of arrangements that can be made during buyer-seller negotiations (see Table 7.3).

Concessions made on minor points can, over time, actually improve the business relationship. This happens when sellers protect the interests of buyers while accomplishing their own goals. Making concessions requires you to view particular transactions in a more creative way, and it may require that you invest in different options from those that were first considered. For example, to sell a *total* solution, you may engage in a partnership with other suppliers to better service customers. This is done frequently in technology sales, where hardware companies partner with software manufacturers to bring a total technology solution to buyers.

TABLE 7.3 Aspects of Products That Can Be Negotiated

- Customer wants the design in eight weeks; it better suits your schedule to make it in six or ten weeks. If the customer changes, can you?

- The prospect wants the equipment in six months; you would prefer to ship it in five months. This could be a negotiation point.

- The customer wants exclusive truck shipment; you prefer rail. Which is better?

- The prospect prefers special packaging (cardboard carton shipment, one to a box); you prefer barrel shipment, three to a barrel. How is price affected by type of shipment?

- You prefer to offer design sketches for engineering review; your customer wants full-size drawings. Can this be a negotiating point?

- Installation time and on-site training programs can vary; these are negotiable points.

- The prospect changes specifications after the order is placed and released for manufacture. How will these be charged back?

- Will shipping costs be paid by the seller or the buyer?

- Order placement time is the best time to get a replacements parts order. A good parts order can be very profitable.

(continued)

TABLE 7.3 Aspects of Products That Can Be Negotiated (*continued*)

- Basic price: This is probably the item most often negotiated. Continually sell value by emphasizing the benefits of your products/services. If there are any "gives" in this area, you must get something in return, such as a change in shipping schedule, payments schedule, parts order, specifications, and/or purchase order.

- FOB (freight on board) point: Ownership of material can pass at the shipping or receiving point. Processing claims for possible shipping damages between these points takes time and effort and must be initiated by the owner at the time of damage. On overseas shipments, ports of embarkation, ship designation, and export clearances are all topics for discussion and negotiation.

- Special warranties and guarantees: The length of time a product is guaranteed can vary. It can start from the time it leaves the factory to after it is in service for a period of time. You can consider extended periods of coverage following the normal guarantee. Does your standard policy cover only the repair or replacement of the defective part? What about cost of removal, packing, and reinstallation of the defective product? What about loss of revenue while a product is out of service? Is it feasible to supply a "loaner?" All of these areas are negotiable.

- Payments: When will payment be made? At shipment, upon receipt, ten or thirty days after installation, after in-service, after six months? Is there a discount? On large projects or major purchases, should progress payments be made? What's the schedule? Who should decide on progress?

- Delays: If the project is delayed beyond the shipping date by the seller, buyer, someone else, or something else, how will the cost be handled? What about storage—who will pay? How much for how long? What about extra handling or loss of revenue by the buyer?

- Cancellation Charges: What portion of total cost will be charged to the buyer if he cancels before shipment? The charge can range from a minimum cancellation charge to 100 percent of the order, depending on the engineering, design, manufacturing, and testing completed. When capital equipment is ordered, many actions begin before the manufacturing starts. Materials must be ordered, designs started, tools set aside, financing arranged, and so on. If an order is canceled, the seller has a right to recoup expenditures. Of course, if manufacturing has already started, additional expenditures are involved. How much the seller is entitled to in the event of a cancellation is a negotiable item.

When to Walk Away

There are times when both parties disagree and walk away from unpromising negotiations. When this happens, it is important that both sides remain professional. As a general rule, it is helpful for businesspeople to establish in advance at what point they will walk away. By predetermining the types of concessions they are willing to make and the absolute lowest offer they are willing to accept—and sticking to those things—both parties can walk away without feeling as though they have lost anything. Although parties may disagree during a particular negotiation, this does not necessarily mean that the relationship dissolves. Often such relationships are reconciled and become very successful partnerships.

There are obvious reasons to break off negotiations—for example, the final best offer is not acceptable, a better alternative is found, or something seriously disturbing is uncovered about the other party. There are also subtler, more subjective reasons for leaving the negotiating table. The negotiator who takes pride in making the unworkable work should pay special attention to the following warning signs[2]:

- The opponent is simply too difficult.
- Transactional costs are too high.
- The negotiator feels the need to teach someone a lesson.
- The negotiator's gut tells her to walk away.

Motivational Selling

Once you have handled the prospect's objections and the prospect has agreed with the evidence you have provided, it is time to motivate the prospect. It is time to move the prospect toward that all-important decision: *Buy now!* Using motivational selling, you will ask the prospect a preselected set of questions to determine his dominant buying urge, which directs and determines his thinking and actions. You can then use this knowledge to show him how buying the product or service will help to satisfy that dominant buying urge.

At this stage you are *motivating*, not reasoning, and *stimulating*, not debating. You already have credibility; now reach for something to overcome the last barrier. You want the prospect to start enjoying right now, at least vicariously, the benefits of the product or service. You want the prospect to see for himself that promotion he could get (which he expects to receive if his department reaches a new goal); you want him to visualize reporting to the board of directors on the big profitability increase that his department is going to achieve because of the product or service. This is what motivation is all about. It is a matter of finding out what turns people on, and then *turning them on.*

First, however, you have to discover the prospect's motivator. You have not sold anything until you have detected the real reason behind why the prospect *needs*—or *wants*—what you are selling.

The RAP Method

Use the RAP method to craft the motivation step in the sales presentation. This method includes the following elements:

1. *R: Reviewing* the problem.
2. *A: Answering* the prospect's questions.
3. *P: Projecting* the prospect as a satisfied customer by painting a mental image of the prospect using the product.

Then comes the wrap-up—the trial close.

Reviewing the Problem

You should practice using the RAP formula. Don't be afraid of sounding corny. Repeat out loud: "The thing I want most in the world is . . ." It may be a new home, a business of your own, to travel around the world, a dignified retirement, a promotion, a specific position or title, educated and successful children, or to be debt-free. Choose it, make it personal, and make it specific.

You should conduct the same type of review for prospects. Review what each prospect wants most. For example, "Mr. Temple, you said that what you want most from the vendor who supplies you is . . ."

Answering the Prospect's Questions

You can answer prospects' questions as outlined earlier in this chapter. You should confirm your understanding of what the prospect says she wants most.

Projecting the Prospect as a Satisfied Customer

In order to learn to project, use visualization. You should first practice on yourself by imagining that you suddenly have what you want—your dreams have come true! Then ask yourself the following questions:

- Exactly what do I see in my mind's eye as I imagine enjoying my dreams come true? (It is a beautiful picture, isn't it?)
- What am I hearing in my mind's ear? Who is saying what and to whom? (These sounds are music to the ears, since they are what you want to hear!)
- What sensations of touch, taste, and smell does my mind conjure up as I reflect on the achievement of my goal? What does my imagination let me taste, touch, and smell as I mentally enjoy my newly achieved success?

Prospects also want something. They also dream of achieving certain things. You can help prospects to achieve their goals. When you describe prospects as satisfied customers who have attained what they want, prospects love you for it! For example, if you are selling medical equipment, there are several ways in which you might help a prospect project. You might paint a picture of improved patient health that results from better diagnostics, or paint a financial picture using the customer's financial operations as a basis for showing improved revenue or cost positions as a result of the equipment purchase. You also might paint a picture of hospital personnel feeling good about their jobs because they are able to provide improved health care for their patients.

Similarly, you can ask prospects/customers to visualize success resulting from purchasing the product or service. Focus your questions on getting prospects to think about accomplishing both their personal *and* professional goals.

Imaginative Visualization and Creative Imagery

Through imaginative visualization and creative imagery, you can help your prospects anticipate how they will use and enjoy products/services. You can make prospects *feel*. You can make them *want*. And you can make them *act*.

The mental images or word pictures you create for prospects do not have to be elaborate and involved to be effective. For example, "Mr. Moore, I appreciate your candid responses to my questions concerning the growth goals for your company, and I look forward to seeing you and your staff at the radio remote broadcast as we welcome hundreds of people to your new store. We will give out tickets to the upcoming concert, bumper stickers, and other door prizes. More importantly, the store traffic generated during the broadcast will more than pay for the cost of your radio campaign." You've put the prospect mentally at the grand opening of his new store; in his mind, the prospect is already reaping the benefits of the radio campaign as a satisfied customer. If a prospect mentally sees himself owning and enjoying the product or service, you are well on the way to a sale.

In selling, the benefits or end results of the product or service (especially an intangible one) always happen in the future. They must. How can the prospect physically enjoy the benefits of the product or service unless the prospect *buys* it? You cannot control the actual future experience that will arouse joy or fear, satisfaction or anxiety in the prospect as a result of the product or service. However, you can control, produce, or create a mental image in the prospects' mind that will arouse similar emotions. You can mentally transport prospects into the future and let them enjoy the end results of the product or service before buying it. In fact, you direct the powerful influence of prospects' emotions and basic instincts, which are what motivates prospects to take action and buy from you, the agile salesperson.

Using the RAP Method Effectively

Using the RAP method effectively involves many factors, including empathy, creative imagination, and enthusiasm. Following are definitions and explanations to help clarify these terms:

- *Empathy.* Remember, this is the most important characteristic of a salesperson. Empathy is the ability to mentally put yourself in the other person's place—to look at that person's situation through her eyes. This helps you develop a feel for the situation, an understanding that the prospect will sense and trust, and it puts you in the right frame of mind. This is an ideal selling attitude.
- *Creative imagination.* This term refers to the ability to create mental images or pictures of things not yet in existence. To mentally transport prospects into the future, picture your own mental and physical reactions in your own mind. Only then are you ready to transfer those mental images from your mind to the prospects' mind.
- *Enthusiasm.* The word *enthusiasm* comes from the Greek words *en theos* and means "God within us." The modern connotation is "fer-

vor, zeal, intensity of expression." Many people confuse enthusiasm with noise or animation. Animation is body movement and can be done without enthusiasm. One can have animation without enthusiasm, but one cannot have enthusiasm without animation. When people become enthusiastic, they get excited, and this excitement usually results in bodily action or animation. If you are sincerely interested in prospects and excited about the value and benefits of your products, your enthusiasm will show. The key to this, however, is sincerity. Being insincere and exhibiting false excitement will appear ridiculous. Remember: Emotions arouse, sustain, and direct human behavior.

A Complete Unit of Motivation in Action

The following is a complete scenario demonstrating the motivation step in action. Notice how the the RAP method is incorporated. This method is the key that can help you motivate your prospects to *want* what you are selling.

> Mr. Ogden, I believe that you did say, earlier in the interview, that you want your employees to be more satisfied on the job. Did I understand you correctly? And you have wanted an answer [problem review]. Well, this is it! [Then you present your answer.]

> If you buy our office products, then here's what will happen. A year from now [projecting to a specific time], you are in your office and overhear your employees saying that the office products you've been buying have made their jobs easier. Mr. Ogden, this is a step toward enhancing employee morale. What do you think?

> I would like to go ahead and get the office products delivered to you next week and get your employees on the road to more job satisfaction. That's what you really want, isn't it?

The phrase, "That's what you really want, isn't it?" is very powerful and effective when used properly. However, it should be used only once during the sales interview, and then only after you have finished creating a mental image in the prospect's mind. The phrase has a tremendous effect on the prospect because you use it at the exact psychological moment when the prospect's mind and emotions will accept a subtle suggestion. It is also a closing question. *If you get a positive reaction from the prospect when using this phrase, you should ask for the order immediately, and the transaction can be closed at this point.*

Trial Close Again

After answering all the prospect's questions and concerns, it is time to trial close again. You can ask the prospect any of the following questions: "What do you think?" "How does all of this sound?" "How do you feel about what I've said so far?" If you get a positive reaction at this point it is time to ask for the order.

The climax of a sales presentation is the completion of the presentation. Once you have pointed out the problem, prescribed how a product or service will solve that problem, and presented the terms of the sale, it is time for you to ascertain whether the relationship will proceed with or without a transaction. The key to completion is for you to make sure that you know where the prospect stands when the presentation is over. The next chapter on completion and partnering provides some ideas on how to get the prospect/customer to consummate the deal and begin the business relationship.

8 *Completion and Partnering*

> We attach a great deal of importance to humility and honesty; with respect for
> human values, we promise to serve our customers with integrity.
> —Azim Premji

The Completion and Partnering Steps

Historically, academics and practitioners have taught selling as more of a transactional approach—as how to get to the "close." The traditional close has dramatically changed. There are multiple closes along a relationship spectrum as salespeople strive to reach the ultimate trusted advisor status, whereby the customer completely trusts the salesperson, her product and service solutions, the selling company and its network of relationships with suppliers.

Traditionally, the close has been the logical conclusion of a sales presentation—the time following a complete, professional sales presentation when the customer decides either to buy now, buy later, or not buy at all. But the close is more than that. It is really an attempt to complete the transaction and open the relationship. In other words, what traditionally has been referred to as the "close" is actually an "open"—the time to *complete the transaction* and the opportunity to *open the door* to what could be a mutually profitable, long-term business relationship: *a partnership*. This is an important distinction and a mindset change for most salespeople. If you take the perspective of building a long-term partnership with a business prospect, it changes your approach to the sales call and your behaviors throughout the relationship-building process.

A *closing mentality* focuses strictly on the transaction as the end result of a sales presentation. A *completion mentality* emphasizes the point that all sales presentations must reach some type of conclusion, but realizes that the conclusion of a presentation may or may not be the close. On average, it takes five sales calls on a business prospect to complete a transaction. Today, more and more salespeople are engaging the customer over multiple sales calls, not one-time transactions. The science of selling is an ongoing process, not one that starts and ends.

A *partnering mentality* changes the salesperson's primary goal from one of simply completing the transaction to that of beginning a partnership with the prospect. Ultimately, the goal is to be viewed as a consultant, a trusted business advisor—as someone who solves customers' business issues and inspires business performance. When operating in this mindset, the partnership actually begins long before the close. The foundation of your relationship with the prospect is established as you spend time on prospecting, preparing, and making the presentation. This is the optimal manner in which to approach a relationship with the prospect, and it is the mentality that you are encouraged to adopt. Some buyers will be insulted if you take their time and do not pay them the courtesy of asking for a decision (hopefully a sale), so you should always ask for a decision. The close of a presentation often represents the invitation by a prospect to the salesperson to continue the relationship. Consider the outcomes of a presentation:

- A prospect buys and becomes a customer—there is more work to be done.
- A customer buys again (rebuy situation)—there is more work to be done.
- A customer or prospect makes no purchase but requests additional information—there is more work to be done.
- A prospect expresses no interest in working with the salesperson's company—there is still more work to be done.

In other words, regardless of the outcome of any one sales presentation, there is more work to be done, and that means that completing a presentation really represents an opportunity for you to learn and act. Over time, a "no" can turn into a "yes." Why? Because customers' needs change.

A Closing Mentality

In traditional sales language, *closing the sale* refers to the salesperson asking the buyer for an order. A *closing question* is one that asks for a definite, immediate decision. All closing strategies are predicated on triggering an answer from a prospect—a decision to buy, a reason for not buying, or a request for additional information.

The Nature of the Traditional Sales Close

If you asked a hundred salespeople to state their greatest problem in selling, the majority would probably say, "I have trouble with closing and knowing where I stand after I leave the prospect's place of business." Yet most of that group could not tell you why this is true. A real issue in closing is the anxiety, hesitancy, or inability of human beings to make decisions. Surprisingly, most salespeople are afraid of rejection. Their minds sometimes jump to possible negative consequences, creating a negative attitude.

However, at this stage of the sales process, you should rejoice. Think about it. You have made it through all the previous steps. Now comes the celebration. Completing the transaction should be the easiest of all steps in the process. It's the next logical thing to do. So you should be positive and confident, especially at this stage. When it's time to close, do the following: *Look, Lower, Lean, Shut Up, Nod, and Smile.*

1. *Look* the prospect/customer directly in the eye. This commands attention.
2. *Lower* your voice. This produces a sense of confidentiality, which is what Alfred Hitchcock meant when he said, "You can make the American public believe anything if you tell them softly enough."
3. *Lean* closer to the prospect/customer. This is another way to stimulate a sense of confidence.
4. *Shut up.* After asking for the order, let the prospect/customer be the next person to speak.
5. *Nod* your head "yes." Be affirmative.
6. *Smile!* Be pleasant. Nobody wants to make a serious decision unless they can be comfortable while doing it.

Traditional Closing Techniques

In this section, we present an overview of some closing techniques commonly used by salespeople. You can use more than one technique during a presentation. You should pick the ones with which you feel more comfortable.

Many prospects find it difficult to make a decision, especially when a substantial monetary commitment is involved. The prospect wants to make the right decision, but complete certainty in buying never exists. If you let them, many prospects thus will postpone decisions. They feel the need to sort and arrange all the pros and cons of your offer. They want to be objective, but they struggle with the emotions associated with the risk of buying. After a sales presentation, prospects often feel confused and hesitant. Your goal is to explain or demonstrate how your product or service benefits outweigh the risks associated with buying. See Table 8.1 for a listing of some popular closing techniques.[1]

TABLE 8.1 Popular Closing Techniques

Closing techniques are prescribed actions salespeople take to persuade the customer to make the necessary commitment. Here are some popular ones:

Adjournment Close	• Give them time to think.
Alternative Choice Close	• Give them a choice involving two minor points (Minor Points Close).
Alternative Source Close	• Become first choice for second place.
Ask for the Order Close	• Ask directly for the sale (Directive Imperative Close).
Ask the Manager Close	• Use your manager as authority to offer more.
Assumptive Close	• Act as if they are ready to decide.
Best Time Close	• Emphasize how now is the best time to buy.
Bracket Close	• Make three offers with the target in the middle.
Calculator Close	• Use a calculator to present the savings.
Calendar Close	• Put a date in calendar to revisit.
Continuous Yes Close	• Keep asking questions that produce a continuous positive response.
Customer Care Close	• Have the customer care manager call later and reopen the conversation.
Daily Cost Close	• Reduce cost to a daily amount.
Economic Close	• Show how the cost is less by considering certain economic factors.
Emotion Close	• Trigger identified emotions.
Extra Information Close	• Give them more info to tip them into closure.

TABLE 8.1 Popular Closing Techniques (*continued*)

Fire Sale Close	• Clearance goods, greatly discounted.
Future Close	• Close on a future date.
Golden Bridge Close	• Make the only option attractive.
Handover Close	• Have someone else do the final close.
Handshake Close	• Offer a handshake to trigger automatic reciprocation.
Never the Best Time Close	• Reframe their reasons for procrastinating.
No Hassle Close	• Make it as easy as possible.
Opportunity Cost Close	• Show the cost of not buying.
Ownership Close	• Act as if they own what you are selling.
Power Question Close	• Ask for the "real" objection.
Price Promise Close	• Promise to match any other price.
Probability Close	• Ask what the probability of doing business is.
Quality Close	• Sell on quality, not on price.
Retrial Close	• Go back to square one.
Reserve an Advantage Close	• Reserve a few extras to offer as a bonus (Extra Bonus Close).
Save the World Close	• Buy now and money goes to charity.
Shopping List Close	• Tick off a list of their needs.
Similar Situation Close	• Bond them to a person in a story.
Single Benefit Close	• Stress the benefit that cannot be matched by competition.
Standing Room Only Close	• Buy now before the opportunity changes.
Suggestion Close	• Give a recommendation.
Summarize the Benefits Close	• Recap the benefits of the offering point by point.
Take Away Close	• Take away the benefit, then give it back.
Testimonial Close	• Use a happy customer to convince the prospect.
Total Cost of Ownership Close	• Compare cost over time with competitors.
Treat Close	• Persuade them to "give themselves a treat."
Trial Close	• Test if they are ready for a close.
Trial Order Close	• Offer a small order on a trial basis.
Valuable Customer Close	• Offer them a special "valued customer" deal.
Weighing Close	• Weigh the facts for buying versus not buying.

Source: Changing Minds website, "Closing Techniques" (2001-11), http://changingminds.org/disciplines/sales/closing/closing_techniques.htm

Here are some traditional closing techniques you can use:

Ask for the Order Close

This approach is also known as the *direct imperative*. Most prospects do not volunteer to buy, even when they have made up their mind to do so. You must lead them. There are a number of skillful ways of asking for the order. "Do you want this thing?" is probably not going to be as effective as "When do you think your purchasing people can have a purchase requisition ready on this?" or "Well, that seems to cover everything. You can initial your acceptance right here." Here are a few other ways to ask directly for the order.

- "Should I put you down for 200 units?"
- "Would you like to okay this order?"
- "May I have your permission to place your order with our shipping department today?"
- "I have your specs already written up. May I get your signature approving what we discussed today?"

There are many situations in which prospects are waiting for you to ask them to buy. For example, the prospect may have raised some straightforward business objections. Once you have responded satisfactorily, you can ask directly for the sale. This approach is especially effective with prospects that have certain social styles, such as drivers, who like a direct approach.

Assumptive Close

This closing approach is particularly useful after you have asked a couple of trial close questions. Assume that the prospect has accepted all your recommendations and that she wants to buy. *Assumptive closes* take shape in the form of questions that do not relate to the product itself. Below are some examples.

- "Mr. White, our payment terms are 2/10, net 30. However, this month I can extend the terms to net 45. May I go ahead and place the order for you?"

- "Ms. Willis, which of our payment plans do you prefer?"
- "Ms. Smith, how would you like this shipped?"
- "Mr. Welsh, when do you usually receive shipment?"
- "How many people would you want to send to our free post-installation maintenance seminar?"
- "What accessories do you want us to ship with the original equipment?"

Assuming a sale is a natural reaction to a good sales presentation; it shows your conviction in your products. If prospects are not ready to buy, the worst that can happen is they will say "no." At that point, you ask more questions to engage the prospect again.

Alternative Choice Close

This closing technique is very effective because it makes it easy for the prospect to make a small decision. The basic psychology behind this strategy is that it does not represent a choice between buying and not buying. The less serious the facts or conditions involved, the less emotional strain on the prospect, and therefore the easier the decision.

When using this technique, you are assuming that the prospect is going to buy but is reluctant to make the final decision. You should therefore give her a choice of quantity, quality, delivery dates, colors, textures, or other details about the product. Have the prospect make a small decision involving two minor points or facts. For example:

- "Would you prefer our two-year or three-year payment plan?"
- "Would you want delivery three or four times annually?"
- "Would you prefer that the first shipment come in July or August?"
- "Would you prefer rail or truck shipment?"
- "When would you want to inspect the equipment in our plant, next week or next month?"

This closing strategy always gives the customer an alternative. It also communicates the fact that you are thinking about the customer's situation and are willing to go the extra mile to demonstrate creative and innovative ideas.

Summarize the Benefits Close

If a presentation is well done, you may *summarize the benefits* of your offering point by point, especially if during the presentation the prospect has agreed with your statements about product/service benefits.

Summary slides are useful tools here. Generally, it is wise to start the summary with a benefit with which it is easy for the prospect to agree. This opening benefit is then followed by a summary of several other benefits.

> Mr. Petsch, I'd like to summarize our discussion at this point. The use of our *(product feature)* will allow you to stay ahead of your competition. It will also help cut your expenses, increase the morale of your employees, and reduce your downtime for repairs."

Following the summary of benefits, you should proceed immediately to the closing question. This technique is especially useful for experienced salespeople who have developed a strong relationship with the buyer.

Weighing Close

The *weighing close* permits you to help the prospect reach an objective decision based on the available facts and evidence at hand. When using the weighing close don't oversell—remember, your goal is to become a trusted advisor.

You may need to assist the prospect in weighing the ideas for buying versus not buying. Help the prospect reach a favorable buying decision by weighing the ideas and facts so that those in favor of buying outweigh those opposed to buying. The weighing close (or *pros and cons close,* as it is often called) tends to be believable to the prospect only if salespeople are objective and honest in admitting that there are two sides to be considered. Below are the nine steps involved in the weighing close.

Step 1: Use Introductory Phrases

- "Mr. Ortega, you haven't missed many opportunities or you wouldn't be where you are today. I would like to get your input on what we've discussed. What do you see are the benefits in what I'm offering, and what are the risks?"

- "Mrs. Clemmons, in your position I know that you are constantly called upon to make decisions and that you like to have all the facts in front of you to intelligently weigh all the available information in making a decision. So, why don't we simply list the ideas opposed and ideas in favor and see how we stand?"

Step 2: Draw the "T" and Label It

- "So that we can be more objective, let's just draw a balance sheet and list the ideas opposing this solution and the ideas in favor of it and see how they stack up."

Step 3: List All of the Prospect's Ideas Opposed to Purchasing

- "You mentioned a few minutes ago that you were concerned about . . ."

As you list the ideas opposed to purchase, write them down on the left side of your balance sheet so your prospect can see them as he hears you say, "Now I believe you mentioned that your budget has been cut. So getting the best value for the money is very important to you. Isn't that true? Is there anything else?"

Step 4: Ask Three Times for Other Ideas Opposed

- "In addition to these ideas, are there any other ideas opposed that you can think of?"
- "Is there anything else that would cause you to hesitate now?"
- "In other words, these are the only ideas opposed to making a positive decision, right?"

Step 5: List Both the Prospect's and Your Ideas in Favor

- "On the other side here, under the ideas in favor, you mentioned that you did like . . . "
- "Well, let's review the reasons why you should start this program now."

Step 6: Make Your Last Positive Idea One That Appeals Strongly to the Prospect's Dominant Buying Urge

- "And most important of all . . ."
- "Last, and most important, you will be able to resell the best product on the market. You'll gain market share and you will have the satisfaction of knowing that your customers will come back to your store, because *they* are satisfied."

Step 7: Review Both Sides of the "T"

- "Now let's take a second look and recheck. We have over here under ideas opposed . . . and over here under ideas in favor . . ." [as you verbally review each item, make a check mark by it].

Step 8: Weigh the Balance

- "Mrs. Patton, I think you'll agree that the ideas in favor outweigh the ideas opposed."

Step 9: Ask for a Favorable Decision

- "Mrs. Hanson, doesn't it just make sense to stock this product before the price increases?"

Remember, as you are using the weighing close, you are getting the prospect/customer to visualize a scale in which the benefits outweigh the costs.

Probability Close

"I need some time to think it over." This objection sets off the panic alarm in salespeople. You can initiate the *probability close* by agreeing with the prospect. You might say, "That will be fine, Ms. Estes. I want you to be comfortable with your decision. Before I call on you again, I'd like to ask you one question. On a hundred-point scale, what do you think is the probability that you will be doing business with my firm?"

Now the ball is in the prospect's court. A sale has not been made . . . yet. Here's how the prospect's responses can be interpreted. Some prospects will be almost certain that they will do business with you; there's only a small chance that they will not. Prospects in this group are almost ready to buy, and you should not pressure them. If you have made an effective presentation, and the prospect has agreed that the product can satisfy his needs in a superior way to competitors, you will not likely lose the sale. Here, high-pressure tactics may get you a short-term sale and lose any long-term relationship/partnering potential.

Some prospects will say there is a 50/50 chance of buying. Many times when prospects want to think about a decision, it is not because they want to delay the decision indefinitely. It may be because they don't completely understand the presentation. You might begin by asking, "What is the probability against purchasing?" The prospect will give an answer, which can be followed with, "What is your reason for that probability?" The prospect's response will allow them to focus on the real objection. You might need to probe, but once the objection is clear, the objection may be converted into a reason for buying, either now or later.

Finally, some prospects will indicate a less than 50 percent chance that they will do business with your firm. In this situation, you may have to start the sales process from the beginning. You can begin by asking for a reason for the low probability. You must remember you are dealing with objections; the situation may be only a reflection of incomplete information.

Power Question Close

This is an extremely effective closing technique, which consists of a simple question: "Is there any *real reason* why you shouldn't buy this right now?" You must give the prospect time to answer. There is great shock power in this question. The prospect can do only two things, buy or voice an objection. The decision has been placed squarely on the prospect.

Customers who like to be challenged are good candidates for this strategy. However, this approach can appear to be manipulative if you have conducted a poor sales presentation. To avoid the feelings of manipulation, you must observe your prospects' nonverbal behavior and pay close attention to projecting sincerity when you ask this question.

Continuous Yes Close

Sometimes you may find it useful to plan a presentation so that the prospect is agreeing with you throughout the presentation.

Salesperson: "That is an attractive feature, isn't it?"

Prospect: "Yes, it is."

Salesperson: "And you can certainly use the extra markup, can't you?"

Prospect: "Well, naturally I can."

Salesperson: "Would it help to get a shipment here in time for your store's next sale?"

Prospect: "Sure."

Salesperson: "Then I had better call the order in, rather than mailing it through normal channels; don't you think?"

Prospect: "Yes."

The *continuous yes* close reduces the buying decision to a series of smaller, easier-to-reach decisions. The idea behind this method is to keep asking questions that will produce "yes" answers from a prospect until the very end of a presentation. The theory, based on positive inertia, is that a prospect will become so accustomed to responding positively to small questions and comments that he will be conditioned to answer "yes" when asked to buy. If you are discussing legitimate features and benefits, you have simply formalized the process of reaching an agreement with the buyer.

The continuous-yes strategy is useful with prospects who have difficulty making decisions. However, too many "yes" responses can become redundant and may even be counterproductive to a successful close. Again, you must observe the prospect's gestures and facial expressions and listen for voice tones to detect whether there is any customer resentment to this technique. Even when you can offer prospects a more profitable approach to their business, you can lose the sale by appearing to be too high-pressure oriented.

Standing Room Only Close

This is a strategy used when demand for a product is high. It is used to convey the same type of feelings as the statement, "There are no seats left; there is standing room only." This close can be used legitimately if the circumstances described are true. Often, price increases, changes in service or delivery, and other events are known well in advance. "We're facing an across-the-board price increase in two weeks. You can save . . . if you buy now. Other customers are capitalizing on the lower price now, and I want to be sure we get your order in while we still have enough product." It is certainly appropriate to offer existing customers an opportunity to buy before buying circumstances change. Many customers do not want to be left out; nor do they want to lose something.

Take Away Close

This is an emotional close. It builds upon a prospect's fear of loss because of indecision. People are afraid of passing up a bargain or missing out on a sure-fire deal. Sometimes you can dramatize the importance of a benefit by taking it away from a prospect and then giving it back. When prospects realize that they may lose the benefit, some may become eager to buy.

Reserve an Advantage Close

Inexperienced salespeople are inclined to build as strong a case as possible by listing every possible product advantage, but sometimes it is helpful to hold a few benefits in reserve. But when the prospect gives a resistance signal, such as hesitating or fretting ("Gee, I really just don't know about this"), you may be able to close right then if you have something more to offer. You might say something like, "I don't believe I mentioned to you that on an order this size, we pay all shipping charges," or "By the way, we also include free delivery."

This approach appeals to the customer's desire to make sound purchase decisions. But it should be used as a last-resort closing strategy. The inducement may be the only way to get the order, but some prospects may perceive it as pressure; they may question why the advantage was not mentioned earlier in the presentation. Moreover, if you use this approach, you have to give something here. By holding something in reserve, you have added value to the product without increasing price.

Single Benefit Close

You may encounter selling situations in which a prospect is excited about a benefit that your competition cannot match. This *single benefit* can be used as the basis to close. "Our company is the only one that can provide you with [the benefit]. When would be a good time for delivery?" You must satisfy the prospect that this is the best decision to make, ask for the order, and promise to *ensure* that the prospect gets the results and benefits expected.

Similar Situation Close

In this closing technique, you present a situation that another prospect faced and describe how it was handled. The key to using this close is to pick a situation that has *similar circumstances*. A story about a person or company that the prospect respects and relates to can be very effective. For example:

> Mr. Burbridge, I would like to show you the results that Company X obtained. You can see how your company would also benefit from using [the product].

Total Cost of Ownership Close

Many times, you can frame a higher price by considering all the costs associated with not making a buying decision. This is particularly true when the prospect is interested but apparently can't justify the financial outlay. Assume a prospect has budget approval of $95,000 for equipment, but the asking price is $102,000. The total cost of ownership close might proceed in the following manner:

> Mrs. Tempton, the difference of $7,000 over your budget approval level presents a small percentage increase for a product with all our features and customer benefits. Over the expected twenty-year life span of the product, that's $350 a year or less than $7 per week—only about $1 per day. Considering the

benefits we discussed in terms of how this solution will reduce your other costs over time, I suggest we move ahead so you can enjoy the many benefits of our product now for only $1 per day over what you anticipated.

Suggestion Close

The *suggestion close* attempts to get prospects to accept a recommendation without a great deal of thought. But this must be done only if the right circumstances exist. Generally, this approach can be used effectively with prospects who face many choices and have little experience with the product or service. You might say something like the following:

> Many customers like you have decided to buy our [product]. They have been quite satisfied with their choice.

The indirect nature of the suggestion close approach allows prospects to feel that they are making their own decision. Testimonials, guarantees or warranties, and contrast statements ("compare ours to . . .") are all good sources of suggestion closes. Most prospects react positively to this type of close because of its low-pressure feel.

Alternate Source Close

Sometimes prospects like to keep all their eggs in one basket, so to speak. They give 100 percent of their business to one supplier. This is risky business. Isn't it better to have a backup in case the supplier fails? That's the thought behind the alternate source close.

> I appreciate the fact that you are satisfied with your present supplier, but wouldn't you agree that there are a few services offered by your present supplier that need improvement? Give us the opportunity to handle this part of your business so that you have the chance to evaluate an alternate source."

As the above implies, this approach is effective with prospects that are fairly satisfied with their present supplier. Suggesting an alternate source offers a low-risk way for the prospect to evaluate a supplier as a possible replacement. You might think of this as being first choice for second place. Over time, taking care of a small portion of the customer's business could lead to a much larger share of his business.

Trial Order Close

As a last resort, you might ask the prospect to accept a small amount of your product or service on a *trial order* or sample basis. Use this technique only after other closing techniques have not succeeded.

The trial order strategy is very useful with most first-time prospects. End-user prospects can purchase and try on a limited basis. It is particularly useful for resellers to see how well the new product sells against existing brands. The reseller will know if the new product sells better by looking at her inventory.

And, of course, smaller orders are better than no order at all. There is value in getting your foot in the door. Small quantities will turn over more quickly than large quantities. Prospects may be more open-minded to a second, larger order because of the fast turnover.

While such an arrangement may be attractive to prospects, you must remember that processing orders is an expensive proposition. Similarly, allowing prospects to test products for a trial period is also expensive. The technique is effective with skeptical prospects, however, so you must weigh the short-term costs against the long-term gains.

The above examples are just a few of many possible closing techniques. They are widely used because they are effective under the right circumstances.

Closing techniques attempt to make it relatively easy for the prospect/customer to decide to buy. If the prospect responds positively, the sale is made. However, it is advisable to be judicious when using traditional closing techniques for the reasons listed in Table 8.2.

A Completion Mentality

Again, a *completion mentality* emphasizes the point that all sales presentations must reach some type of conclusion. However, the conclusion of a presentation may or may not be a transaction. In complex sales situations, it takes engaging the customer over multiple sales calls to get to the transaction state. The importance of developing relationships cannot be overestimated. After all, you are the primary contact with the customer. Thus, you are responsible for implementing your company's customer relationship management (CRM) program. Let's take a look at the possible

TABLE 8.2 Cautions in Using Traditional Closing Techniques

- A badly timed or misstated close can lose a sale and destroy a relationship.

- Partnering with large customers involves much more than the use of high-pressure techniques.

- When salespeople use recognizable closing techniques on veteran buyers, they are less likely to buy. They do not want to be pressured; they want to make decisions that will be in the long-term best interests of their firms.

- Customers who feel pressured or manipulated to make an initial purchase are much less likely to purchase again from the same salesperson and supplying firm.

- Prospects know that many salespeople are eager for a quick sale. They are aware and suspicious of salespeople who use "closing techniques" in a manipulative way. These prospects will rarely agree to buy if they feel pressured to make a decision. They must be comfortable with the salesperson and what he has to offer.

- Traditional methods of closing sales are considered pushy by many buyers who wish to avoid risk, who wish to make the right decision, and who are hesitant to change. Traditional closing techniques applied in team-buying situations can sometimes be ineffective because of this.

outcomes of the presentation's conclusion and your responsibilities to the prospect afterward.

If a Sale Is Made

Making a sale is a good feeling. But your duties are not complete. You are responsible for consummating all transactions and beginning the relationship with the customer on a positive note. After a sale, most buyers appreciate you leaving as soon as possible. But you must finish the required business. Here are some things you should be certain to do before leaving the customer who has agreed to the sale.

- Show appreciation for the customer's business, but avoid excessive expressions of satisfaction. Don't gloat.
- Reassure the customer that the decision is a good one.
- Solicit sales leads. A new customer is a good source of leads because he has just purchased.
- Complete all necessary paperwork and finalize the details.
- Be sure to leave with a good understanding of the customer's expectations.

Subsequent sales calls on a customer should begin with a review of what has been accomplished since the last sales call, and then move on to what should be done to make further progress toward the buyer's and seller's mutually agreed-upon goals.

If the Sale Is Not Made

Of course, you cannot expect to make a sale every time. Nor do you have to do so in order to be successful. What success does require is that you be agile and persistent. When a sale is not made, there are still duties to perform, things to learn, and data to analyze and record.

The purpose here—indeed, the major objective of all post-call activity—is to maintain and increase *customer goodwill.* Goodwill is valuable in the long term. It represents the implicit value of the attitudes of customers and prospective customers toward your organization. You are, in many cases, the primary determinant of goodwill. To customers and prospects, you often *are* the selling organization. Therefore, you must focus on maintaining and enhancing goodwill. This has two aspects when the sale is not made: terminating the sales call and possibly providing service.

Terminating the Sales Call

The prospect did not buy. You could not create a match of product offerings and benefits. When nothing seems to work, one of the most damaging things you can do is to drag out the presentation. You must learn to respect the customer's decision and engage in the following activities before making a prompt exit.

1. Accept the prospect's decision graciously. You cannot let your emotions dominate, and you certainly cannot take it personally that a sale was not made this time. The best thing to do is stay courteous and cheerful. Remember, relationships are the focus, and not pressuring the prospect for a short-term transaction may leave the door open for another presentation at a later time.
2. Say "thank you" for the prospect's time and mean it. The prospect spent time and possibly other resources to participate in the sales presentation. And if she didn't buy, the prospect also has very little to show for her efforts at this point.
3. Do everything, both during and after the presentation, to establish

good rapport with the prospect. It might be appropriate to ask for a brief critique of your presentation. "I value your opinion. Would you please tell me where I fell short?" By soliciting the prospect's input, you may be building goodwill, and the prospect's advice may be helpful with future prospects.

4. Finally, do not tarry. Prospects are busy. And salespeople should be, too. There are other prospects to see, reports to write, and so on.

Table 8.3 provides additional questions a salesperson should answer when a sale has not been made.

TABLE 8.3 The Post-Sales Questionnaire

- Were you expected? Was your customer ready to see you?
- What, specifically, did you plan to sell or accomplish?
- What benefits of your proposition did you present?
- What did the customer have to lose by refusing to buy now?
- Was this prospect really qualified in terms of money, authority, and desire (MAD)?
- Did you really talk to the person with the authority to buy?
- Were you courteous and friendly with all your customer's subordinates, but without taking up their time unnecessarily?
- Did your "opening" effectively secure interest? If not, what changes should you make?
- Did you really tell your *whole* story?
- Did you *listen carefully* to what your customer had to say?
- Did you answer all questions to the customer's satisfaction?
- What objections did the customer present, and how did you meet them?
- Did you give up on the customer's first "no," or did you keep on selling? If you kept on selling, how did you override the customer's "no" without being rude?
- Did you criticize the competition?
- Did you get point-by-point agreement as you told your sales story?
- Did you try only one "close" and give up when you failed?
- Did you let the customer "sell" you that she "didn't need it"?
- Do you feel that your presentation was as well organized as it could have been?
- Who was *really* in control of the solicitation?
- Do you feel that you handled the presentation in a professional way, or might there have been a *better* way?
- Did you reach a completion point in the presentation?

Providing Service

Despite not making a sale, there may be situations in which salespeople do not automatically leave. Many selling situations involve repeat business. In such cases, even though the customer does not place an order at that time, he may want a service related to a previous purchase. Remember, salespeople get more when they give more. With existing customers, the salesperson has already agreed to provide such service. Further, good service now may lead to future sales, and poor service may preclude them. Salespeople may be of service in at least four areas:

- Handling complaints
- Order expediting
- Adjustments, returns, and allowances
- Information

Today, more sales companies are exploring hybrid offerings: profitable combinations of goods and services.[2] This is accomplished by first recognizing that your company is really a service company. "The first step in expanding a service capability is to make both [your] company's managers and customers aware of the value provided by existing services."[3]

In summary, there is nothing aggressive or offensive about asking for a decision. You have researched and found prospects who already have a high probability of buying (e.g., prospecting). You've prepared and presented a factual presentation of features, advantages, and benefits designed to meet that specific prospect's needs or wants. If, indeed, a match exists, you should have no need to pressure the prospect to buy, as it would seem there is a possibility of an exchange to mutual advantage. If a match does not exist, you should not pressure the prospect to buy, as it would seem there is no possibility of exchange to mutual advantage. In either case, you and the prospect should be able to maintain friendly relations.

A Partnering Mentality

Partnerships are not built on short-term objectives only. In a partnership, both you and the buyer perceive a need for the relationship, and each values the other. Partnerships provide many benefits, such as quicker response to change, cost savings, agility in meeting customer needs, increases in sales, and quicker identification of problems and opportunities. In spite of these advantages, salespeople can make many mistakes on the way to forging partnerships. These include:

1. *Failing to plan.* You must be able to assess the value of a partnership over the long run.
2. *Creating ideas and solutions with little to no planning.* This can be dangerous in partnership formation, as potential partners want assurance that your creative ideas and solutions will really provide value.
3. *Cutting a deal that favors the selling organization too much.* The focus should be on joint benefits and the co-creation of value.
4. *Partnering in isolation.* An effective partnership requires that you know what is occurring in your own firm—in production, finance, delivery, maintenance—and how to bring these resources together for the client's benefit.
5. *Seeking quick partnerships.* Taking shortcuts, overlooking details, and failing to keep up with new events can undermine a partnership before it ever starts.
6. *Lacking an exit strategy.* Partnerships do not last forever. You must be capable of seeing the warning signs of an eroding relationship and either repair the relationship or end it on a professional level.
7. *Not being able to walk away.* You are under no obligation to enter into a partnership arrangement, no matter how many calls you have made. How many calls is one call too many?

The Nature of Partnering

Partnering is a way of doing business that helps salespeople and buyers work together to achieve mutual and individual goals. A partnership requires complete commitment from both the buyer and seller. This is why traditional closing methodologies, which are transaction-oriented and often pressure the buyer, are not always appropriate in partnerships. A typical partnering relationship has many characteristics, including:

Commitment

You and your customers must commit to a long-term relationship, in which each understands the goals of the other. Each partner also seeks innovative ways to assist each other in goal achievement and gaining competitive advantage. Commitment leads partners to avoid continuously reassessing the relationship, but each partner also has a dedication to continuous improvement and achievement of common goals.

Trust

Your customers recognize that by sharing information, they reduce the amount of control over their respective situations. Partners must also be tolerant of outside contacts (e.g., competing salespeople). If such trust exists, each partner can obtain benefits that would exceed those derived from individual effort. Trust helps to combine the knowledge and resources of the partners and reduce or eliminate adversarial relationships, which reduces opportunism.

Understanding

You and your customers must understand each other's feelings, responsibilities, expectations, and limitations. You must also expect, discuss, and accept divergent points of view. A key aspect of understanding is *interdependence*—the recognition that each partner perceives a need for the relationship, that each partner values the other's contribution of skills, and that the relationship cannot be easily replaced.

Excellence

Partners strive to create the best possible products/services. Partners expect and encourage mutually agreeable levels of excellence as standards for their working relationships. Excellence lowers the potential for conflict by keeping the power on each side balanced. A balance of influences encourages cooperation by focusing attention on mutual interests.

Clear Expectations

You and your customers must communicate expectations, needs, and an agenda that drives mutual participation. When expectations are understood and agreed upon, relationship instability caused by the desire to seek individual goals is lessened.

Mutual Goals

You and your customers should fully articulate your goals for the partnership. Common goals imply shared vision and shared energy towards solving problems and achieving goals. Cooperation is required to achieve mutual goals and encourage the long-term relationship. Cooperation signals that the relationship is important to the partners and that each partner is willing to make sacrifices for the sake of the partnership.

Execution and Responsiveness

Partnering works when you *and* your customer make good on your commitments by doing your jobs in timely ways with each other's goals in mind. Preparation and continual updating of information are critical. Effectiveness of a partnership is concerned with the performance of various tasks and the satisfaction that each partner perceives from the partnership.

Communications

Continuous communication is needed to assess and evaluate progress toward goals and to maintain the integrity of the partnership. Partners must be prepared to act on feedback, especially when it is focused on achieving mutual goals.[4]

Perspectives on Partnering

In order for you to enter into partnerships with customers, you must provide products and/or services that possess competitive value and improve the customer's situation. For example, products or services can add value by reducing a customer's operating costs. You must reduce these costs significantly enough to make a difference. And you must reduce them dependably enough that the savings can be relied on. Similarly, products or services provide value if they help customers increase their profits from sales of their own products. You must increase these profits significantly enough to make a difference, either by permitting the customer to sell greater volume at existing margins or to sell existing volume at greater margins.

For both you and the customer/prospect, a sale represents the first of many decisions involved in the partnership. It is not the end of the buying process or of the selling process; it is the opening, not the close. From the prospect's point of view, a decision to buy involves a change in attitude and/or behavior. The new chemical is cheaper, but will the service be as reliable? The new equipment is faster, but will it require too much maintenance? A decision not to buy suggests that the prospect is not ready to change. Things continue as before. From the perspective of relationships, however, two things are critical. Failure to reach a decision is never fatal, and success is never final.

Because many buyers are seeking long-term relationships with suppliers, it is often more difficult for them to say "yes" than it is to say "no." If the exchange is to be consummated, you must provide leadership to help prospects make decisions. Building relationships involves a shift in emphasis from persuasion to motivation. You must help prospects make the long-term commitment to purchase products or services that satisfy their expressed and implied needs and wants.

Account Management and Partnering

You cannot and should not pursue partnering relationships with every customer with which you transact business. Developing partnerships with all customers is impractical because of time and cost considerations. Thus, you must develop partnership relations selectively. As you focus your efforts, one of your tasks is to extend your account bandwidth in both the transactional *and* partnering directions. Seek to gain competitive advantage by becoming more partnership-oriented and more transaction-oriented, based on the needs and wants of different customers and customer segments. You must be innovative, crafting relationship strategies that most closely meet the requirements of customers.

Initial calls may not lead to sales. Early sales calls, as you have seen, introduce prospects to you, the sales company, the products/services available, and so on. During these early calls, you must get a read on the prospect—does the prospect seem to desire a long-term partnership or a transaction? In nearly all calls, you define customer needs, attempt to match product benefits with needs, and devise a solution for the prospect's situation. As you progress through the various elements of the sales presentation, the prospect is ascertaining the value of your proposition and weighing his options between a partnership, a transaction, or neither. Some prospects become partners over time. Some prospects seek only a transaction, which may occur as a result of one, two, three, four, or more sales calls. When a transaction occurs, it may signal the end of the relationship with you, as some buyers simply wish to buy one time. However, any transaction situation may result in the prospect electing to continue the relationship. For transactional customers, the basis of the relationship is your core product/service. Transaction-focused customers are often most interested in price, so salespeople are faced with the task of *unbundling* product offerings. That is, they meet customer's demands for price by taking away product/service features that the transaction-focused customer does not need or want. Unbundling requires that you have knowledge of the cost structure of each attribute and/or service, as price reductions to customers cannot exceed the cost reductions associated with removal of the feature. For partnership-oriented customers, augmented products are offered; services such as delivery, installation, training, maintenance and technical assistance are added to the core product on an incremental basis. Such *bundling* of product/service offerings is focused on meeting specific customer needs and wants that go beyond the basic capabilities of the *core product*—the basic features and benefits associated with a product or service.

Become the Preferred Supplier

You should always strive to become the preferred, trusted supplier. Build such a high level of goodwill that customers will always think of you and your sales organization first. To accomplish this, you should do the following:

1. Build a reputation for customer service based on trust and dedication.
2. Build goodwill. This requires attention to customer interests. You must keep in touch with customers and recognize that the customer is the company's most important asset.
3. Stay abreast of market conditions, new products or services, industry trends, technical standards, advertisements, and personnel changes.
4. Establish credibility as a consultant in the eyes of customers by using

a conscientious, professional approach to their needs and wants. Continually review the development of your professional sales skills to determine progress being made.

5. Check call frequency to verify that sufficient personal sales calls are being made based on actual or potential business.

6. Report back to your sales organization on any information regarding savings, size, preferred performance, lower cost, convenience, better delivery, or other features or benefits that competitors announce.

7. Remember that you are part of the product or service that is offered to customers. If customers continue to place their faith in you and your company, build on that relationship. You are an integral part of the total package provided to customers.

In conclusion, we have demonstrated that as business becomes more global and complex, some traditional ways of selling are quickly becoming obsolete. Salespeople are boundary spanners, but the boundaries are getting more blurry. In a key account selling situation, for example, the role of the key account manager as the orchestrator of relationships has morphed into not only a relationship manager but also a general business manager, often with profit and loss responsibility.

Serving the client is the mantra of most companies. However, this concept is becoming more challenging to implement. For example, as client companies engage in broader strategic alliances with other companies, the trusted advisor is expected to provide business solutions and insights which often go beyond the salesperson's company's product and service offerings. Motivating internal-to-the-company constituents to see beyond the immediate sale to the broader relationship has become a fundamental activity to being successful in sales today.

"Sales excellence is a highly ambitious goal, but it is achievable. It requires a salesperson whose personal talents and skills match the selling environment in which he or she works, a solid grounding in traditional and non-traditional sales skills, and, most important in today's highly competitive business-to-business markets, a customer-centric approach."[5]

We hope that we have given you the tools in Selling ASAP to accomplish sales excellence as you strive to become a trusted business advisor. In Table 8.4 below is a checklist, which you can use to test the extent to which your customers believe you are a trusted advisor.

TABLE 8.4 Trusted Advisor Checklist

To what extent do your customers agree . . .

- I depend on the advice my salesperson gives me.
- The information my salesperson provides me with is critical to my success.
- The advice my salesperson gives me is always correct.
- The advice my salesperson gives me enables me to meet my personal goals.
- I may not always agree with the advice my salesperson gives me.
- My salesperson and I always agree about the best course of action for my firm.
- I rely on my salesperson for up-to-date information about the products and/or services I purchase from him/her.
- My salesperson is innovative.
- My salesperson likes to try different things.
- My salesperson likes to take chances.
- My salesperson likes to experiment with new ways of doing things.
- My salesperson enjoys finding new solutions for customers.

Source: Eli Jones and Stephanie Mangus, Copyright 2011

You are invited to join the Selling ASAP community at www.selling asap.com. We want to hear from you as you implement the ideas in this book. Here's to your success!

Notes

1. SELLING ASAP

1. Eli Jones, Steven P. Brown, Andris A. Zoltners, and Barton A. Weitz, "The Changing Environment of Selling and Sales Management," *Journal of Professional Selling and Sales Management* 25, no. 2 (2005): 105–11.

2. Harish Sujan, "Optimism and Street-Smarts: Identifying and Improving Salesperson Intelligence," *Journal of Personal Selling & Sales Management* 19 (Summer 1999): 17–33.

3. Benjamin Gilad, *Business Blindspots: Replacing Your Company's Entrenched and Outdated Myths, Beliefs, and Assumptions with the Realities of Today's Markets* (Chicago: Probus, 1994), 4.

4. Adrian Farrell, "An Organizational Intelligence Framework for the Agile Corporation," Woodlawn Marketing Services (2003). Online at: www.worksys.com/agile.htm.

5. Lawrence Chonko and Eli Jones, "The Need for Speed: Agility Selling," *Journal of Personal Selling & Sales Management* 25, no. 4 (2005): 373–84.

6. Herb Greenberg, Harold Weinstein, and Patrick Sweeney, *How to Hire and Develop Your Next Top Performer: The Five Qualities That Make Salespeople Great* (New York: McGraw-Hill, 2001).

2. UNDERSTANDING HOW BUYERS BUY

1. Jagdish Sheth and Banwari Mittal, "Customer Behavior: A Managerial Perspective," chap. 5 in H. A. Murray, *Explorations in Personality* (New York: Oxford, 1938).

2. See Lyle E. Bourne, Jr., and Bruce R. Ekstrand, *Psychology: Its Principles and Meanings* (3rd ed.; New York: Holt, Rinehart, and Winston, 1979), 255–57.

3. Barton A. Weitz, Harish Sujan, and Mita Sujan, "Knowledge, Motivation, and Adaptive Behavior: A Framework for Improving Selling Effectiveness," *Journal of Marketing* 50 (October 1986): 174–91.

4. David W. Merrill and Roger H. Reid, *Personal Styles and Effective Performance: Make Your Style Work for You* (CRC Press, 1981).

5. Sheth and Mittal, "Customer Behavior: A Managerial Perspective."

6. Abraham H. Maslow, *The Farther Reaches of Human Nature* (New York: Viking Press, 1971); Abraham H. Maslow, *Toward a Psychology of Being* (Princeton: Van Nostrand, 1968).

7. Sheth and Mittal, "Customer Behavior: A Managerial Perspective."

3. PREPARATION

1. George Washington Carver, "Iowa Roots, Global Impact: The Life and Legacy of George Washington Carver." Online at: www.blackiowa.org/exhibits/virtual-tour/george-washington-carver/4/.

2. Alexander Graham Bell. Quotationspage.com, Michael Moncur and QuotationsPage.com, 2011. Online at: www.quotationspage.com/quote/33155.html.

3. Jagdish Sheth and Andrew Sobel, *Clients for Life: Evolving from an Expert for Hire to an Extraordinary Advisor* (New York: Simon & Schuster, 2000).

4. See the website for the U.S. Census Bureau at www.census.gov.

4. ATTENTION

1. William Verbeke and Richard P. Bagozzi, "Sales Call Anxiety: Exploring What It Means When Fear Rules a Sales Encounter," *Journal of Marketing* 64 (July 2000): 88–101.

2. Nicole Howatt-Moberg, "The Power of Rapport, the Connection to Sell: Can Rapport Be Taught?" Lecture at University of Central Florida, 2005.

5. EXAMINATION

1. Quoted in Susan Paterno, "The Question Man," *American Journalism Review,* October 2000. Online at: www.ajr.org/Article.asp?id=676.

2. Charles Green, Sandy Styer,and Bob Bowers, "Think More Expertise Will Make You More Trusted? Think Again." Whitepaper, Trusted Advisors, LLC. Online at: trustedadvisor.com/public/files/pdf/TA_White_Paper.pdf.

3. Dale Carnegie, *How to Stop Worrying and Start Living* (1948). Great-Quotes.com, Gledhill Enterprises, 2011. Online at: www.great-quotes.com/quote/1123190.

4. Neil Rackham, *Major Account Sales Strategy* (New York: McGraw-Hill, 1989).

5. *The Competitive Advantage* 17 (5) (Richmond, Va.: Briefings Publishing Group, 2003).

6. Hal Warfield, "FAQs on Listening—'Hey! Are You Listening?'" (August 31, 2002). Online at: www.halwarfield.com.

7. Alvin M. Hattal, "Tough Customers," *Selling Power* (June 2002): 54–59.

8. Ibid.

9. Gerard Gschwandtner, "Reading Your Customers' Buying Signals," from the editors of *Selling Power*. Online at www.sellingpower.com.

10. Ibid.

6. PRESCRIPTION

1. Robert Townsend, *Up the Organization: How to Stop the Corporation from Stifling People and Strangling Profits* (San Francisco: Jossey-Bass, 2007).

2. K. Witte and K. Morrison, "Examining the Influence of Trait Anxiety/Repression-Sensitization on Individuals' Reactions to Fear Appeals," *Western Journal of Communication* 64 (Winter 2000): 1–26; J. F. Tanner, Jr., and J. B. Hunt, "The Protection Motivation Model: A Normative Model of Fear Appeals," *Journal of Marketing* 55 (July 1991): 36–45.

3. Herb Greenberg, quoted in *Selling ASAP: Art, Science, Agility, Performance* (Cincinnati, Ohio: Thomson South-western, 2002), 3.

7. CONVICTION AND MOTIVATION

1. Adapted from N. Tzokas and M. Saren, "Value Transformation in Relationship Marketing," *Australasian Marketing Journal* 7, no. 1 (1999): 52–62.

2. Marc Diener, "Deals Unplugged: Don't Know When to Cut Your Losses and Leave the Negotiating Table? Look for These Telltale Signs," *Entrepreneur Magazine* (August 2003). Online at: www.entrepreneur.com/magazine/entrepreneur/2003/august/63334.html.

8. COMPLETION AND PARTNERING

1. "Closing Techniques" (2001–2011). Online at: changingminds.org/disciplines/sales/closing/closing_techniques.htm.

2. Werner Reinartz and Wolfgang Ulaga, "How to Sell Services More Profitably," *Harvard Business Review*, May 1, 2008.

3. Wolfgang Ulaga and Werner Reinartz, "Hybrid Offerings: How Manufacturing Firms Combine Goods and Services Successfully," *Journal of Marketing*, 75 (6).

4. A. A. Bubshait, "Partnering: An Innovative and Effective Project Organization Concept," *Cost Engineering* 43 (April 2001): 32–37.

5. Howard Stevens and Theodore Kinni, *Achieve Sales Excellence: The 7 Customer Rules for Becoming the New Sales Professional* (Avon, Mass.: Platinum Press, 2006), 220.

Author Biographies

ELI JONES

Eli Jones is the dean of Louisiana State University's E. J. Ourso College of Business and the E. J. Ourso Distinguished Professor of Business. Widely published in major marketing journals, he is also the coauthor of *Strategic Sales Leadership: BREAKthrough Thinking for BREAKthrough Results*. Recognized for innovative research and creative scholarship, Dr. Jones is the recipient of LSU's 2009 Rainmakers Award, acknowledging faculty who demonstrate exceptional academic productivity. Jones's research is primarily focused on issues related to the changing sales force—sales force diversity, sales force change management and sales force technology adoption and performance, salesperson motivation, and buyer-seller relationships. He is listed in *Marquis Who's Who in America, Madison Who's Who,* is a member of the International Who's Who Historical Society, and has been featured in many national publications, including *Sales & Marketing Management, Selling Power, Biz Ed, Business 2.0,* and the *New York Times.*

Dr. Jones has received excellence in teaching awards on the university, national, and international levels. In August 2008, he was honored with the KPMG Ph.D. Project Marketing Doctoral Students Association Award, and in March 2009 he was named a 2009 Mays Business School Outstanding Doctoral Alumnus of Texas A&M University. He has taught strategic selling, advanced professional selling, key accounts selling, and sales leadership at the undergraduate and MBA levels, and has led a Ph.D. seminar on marketing strategy. Before becoming dean, Dr. Jones served as Associate Dean for Executive Education Programs. Prior to that, he was executive director of the Sales Excellence Institute at the University of Houston. He has been a visiting professor at Vlerick Leuven Gent Management

School in Belgium, at Cornell's School of Hotel Administration, and at the Tuck School of Management, Dartmouth; and he has been a member of the Duke Corporate Education Global Learning Resource Network since 2005. Dr. Jones has designed corporate training courses and has taught senior and midlevel executives about leadership, sales strategies, and customer relationship management in Belgium, Dubai, France, Hong Kong, India, Malaysia, Mexico, Trinidad, the United Kingdom, and the United States. He also is a corporate speaker and speaks on internal and external motivation of salespeople, selling strategies, customer relationship management, and sales force leadership.

Before becoming a professor, Dr. Jones worked in sales and sales management for three Fortune 100 companies. Positions held include key account manager, key account executive (responsible for two of the Top 25 accounts in the United States), zone sales planning manager (responsible for sales in three states), sales manager, and zone sales manager designate. He earned his undergraduate, MBA, and Ph.D. degrees from Texas A&M University.

LARRY CHONKO

Lawrence B. Chonko is the Thomas McMahon Professor of Business Ethics at the University of Texas at Arlington. He came to University of Texas–Arlington in 2007 after twenty-two years at Baylor University and seven years at Texas Tech University. Dr. Chonko is the author or coauthor of fifteen books, including *Selling ASAP; Entrepreneurship and Leadership in Business; Creative Entrepreneurship, Direct Marketing, Direct Selling, and the Mature Consumer; Professional Selling; Managing Salespeople; Business, the Economy, and World Affairs* (8 editions); and *Ethics and Marketing Decision Making.* He has also served as editor of the *Journal of Personal Selling and Sales Management.* Author of over two hundred papers, Dr. Chonko has also published articles in the *Journal of Marketing,* the *Journal of Marketing Research,* the *Journal of the Academy of Marketing Science,* the *Academy of Management Journal,* and other leading journals. Throughout his career, Dr. Chonko has served as a consultant to industrial products, consumer products, service, and nonprofit organizations. Dr. Chonko has received several research and teaching awards and conducts research in the areas of professional selling, sales management, change management, and ethics. He is the recipient of the American Marketing Association Sales Interest Group Lifetime Achievement Award for his work in sales and sales force management, the Circle of Honor Award from the Direct Selling Education Foundation, and the "Moon" Mullins Award for service to the Baylor University Bear Foundation. Dr. Chonko earned his Ph.D. from the University of Houston.

FERN JONES

Fern Walker Jones is the life and business partner and first lady of Dean Eli Jones. Referred to by their academic and business colleagues as "Eli's secret weapon," Fern has strategically worked in conjunction with Dr. Jones to build upon a legacy of entrepreneurship and learning. She is creative director and resident editor of the first edition of *Selling ASAP: Art, Science, Agility, Performance,* and coauthor of the professional edition.

Fern's background in service prepared her for a life with the consummate salesman and for raising a household of salespeople. Her diverse background began in 1978 as a prosthetic hair designer, consultant, and trainer for one of the top hair-replacement distributors in Houston, Texas. Later, to accommodate the social and educational needs of her preschool-aged children, Fern changed careers to work for Kindercare, Inc., where she taught preschool and kindergarten. Within a short period, she was promoted to director, acquiring a school in Jacksonville, Florida. Fern received awards and accolades from corporate supervisors, and more importantly from parents, for the exceptional care and education the children received under her management.

Fern moved on to post-secondary education in 1993, and within her first year of employment in the Department of Marketing of the Mays Business School at Texas A&M University, she received the Staff Excellence Award for exceptional service to the college. She also became a self-taught freelance graphics designer, creating presentations for academic and professional speakers, designing marketing collateral for organizations (e.g., the Program for Excellence in Selling and the Sales Excellence Institute at the University of Houston, and The Sales Educators, LLC), and designing class slides for the college textbook divisions of Thomson-Southwestern Learning and McGraw-Hill. Fern later accepted a position with Caldive International (CDI), a leading provider of subsea services to the oil and gas industry, as senior executive assistant to the vice president of major projects; she subsequently became the graphics coordinator for business development, designing and packaging proposals for bid to oil and gas companies, as well as designing executive presentations for top-to-top sales meetings.

In 2000 Fern left corporate to manage two family-owned businesses that she and Eli launched and developed, Eli Jones & Associates, Inc. (EJA), a sales and marketing, executive education, and research firm; and Novewave, LLC (in partnership with Infowave, based in Chennai, India), an innovative multimedia business solutions provider. Together, Eli and Fern have combined their talents to build a platform for Dr. Jones to share his passion for and expertise in sales/strategic sales management to educate and motivate organizations around the world.

CARL G. STEVENS

Carl G. Stevens was charter director of the Center for Professional Selling and Sales Management at Baylor University as well as a member of the advisory board of Baylor University's Hankamer School of Business and the Schools of Business at the University of Houston and Houston Baptist University. More recently, he was chairman of the board for the Institute of Certified Sales Professionals (www.theicsp.com) and the coordinator of intellectual properties at the Institute. Dr. Stevens received the Outstanding Sales Educators Award of the Decade from Texas A&M University. He has coauthored four books in addition to *Selling ASAP,* including *Selling; Agri-Selling; The Secrets of Super Selling: How to Program Your Subconscious;* and *How Winners Win.* He is the creator of the Coaches Clinic, a program geared toward sales managers; he developed the Effective Executive Communication program and workbook, teaching verbal and nonverbal communication for management; he produced *Advanced Studies in Professional Selling,* a workbook with audio; and he is the designer of The iCSP Blueprint for Professional Selling, a seminar about how to structure a complete professional presentation in the proper psychological process for maximum motivational appeal. In addition to these ventures, he has been published in *Sales Management Magazine, Marketing News, Commerce Magazine–San Antonio, Sales and Marketing Council Bulletin, Speakout* (the official publication of the National Speakers Association), the *Houston Chronicle,* and many other publications.

Mr. Stevens has done sales education and consulting projects across six continents and fifty-one countries for companies including Caterpillar, Dresser, Du Pont, Ford Motors, IBM, John Deere, Kodak, Mitsubishi, Prudential, Quaker, RCA, Upjohn, Volkswagen, Westinghouse, Yale, Xerox, and many more. He is considered one of the nation's leading authorities in the field of programmed sales education and human resource development. He has been inducted into the Speakers Hall of Fame and granted the National Speakers Association's Council of Peers Award of Excellence, the highest award in professional speaking, joining ranks with such recipients as President Ronald Reagan and Art Linkletter.

Index